C000121018

# THE QUEEN AND US

# THE QUEEN AND US

*Nigel Nicolson*

Weidenfeld & Nicolson
LONDON

First published in Great Britain in 2003
by Weidenfeld & Nicolson

A CIP catalogue record for this book
is available from the British Library.

ISBN 0 297 82940 8

Typeset by Selwood Systems, Midsomer Norton

Printed in Great Britain by
Butler & Tanner Ltd, Frome and London


Weidenfeld & Nicolson

The Orion Publishing Group Ltd
Orion House
5 Upper Saint Martin's Lane
London, WC2H 9EA

For Juliet

# CONTENTS

# ILLUSTRATIONS

*Between pages 54 and 55:*
King George V preparing to broadcast his Christmas
    message [1]
George V with Princess Elizabeth at Balmoral in 1928 [2]
Princess Elizabeth aged ten [3]
The Duke and Duchess of Windsor on their wedding day
    in 1937 [1]
The royal family in 1942 [3]
George VI's visit to Malta in 1943 [4]
The informal style of the royal family in 1943 [3]
George VI takes the Victory Parade in 1946 [5]
Queen Elizabeth arrives home from Kenya, after the death
    of her father in 1952 [3]
Elizabeth on her way to open Parliament in 1952, after her
    Accession but before her Coronation [5]
The royal family on the balcony of Buckingham Palace
    after the Coronation [1]
Queen Elizabeth leaves No. 10 Downing Street after
    having dinner with Churchill [1]
The Queen's Silver Jubilee in 1977 [3]
Queen Elizabeth with her Commonwealth Prime
    Ministers in 1977, at a banquet to celebrate the Silver
    Jubilee [7]

*Between pages 118 and 119:*
Prince Charles and Lord Mountbatten [1]
Charles and Diana on their wedding day [7]

The author and the publishers offer their thanks to the
following for their kind permission to reproduce images:

1  Camera Press Ltd
2  The Royal Collection (© 2003 HM Queen Elizabeth II)
3  Hulton Getty Images
4  The Illustrated London News Picture Library
5  Popperfoto
6  Rex Features
7  Tim Graham, London
8  Corbis

# I

THE monarchy does not intrude greatly into our lives. A much-praised history of the last century, Noël Annan's *Our Age*, makes no mention of Edward VIII's abdication nor of George VI, and refers only once to our present Queen, praising her for her kindness to John Profumo after his disgrace. But the monarchy is always present in the background. The media remind us of its existence almost every day, and from time to time it emerges into extraordinary prominence – at a coronation, a wedding, a jubilee, a divorce, a parade, a funeral – and depending on the glamour of the occasion and the current popularity of the leading actors, we react, usually with approval, occasionally with indifference, rarely with hostility. Our attitude to the royal family changes with an unpredictability that must be confusing to them. Do we expect them to behave like ordinary people? But they cannot, because we have given them extraordinary roles. In demanding that they bring themselves "up to date" what exactly do we mean? When their private lives occasionally go astray, like the lives of most of us, we complain that they are betraying royalty's mystique. One purpose of this book is therefore to enquire what we demand of the royal family, how far they fulfil it, and how they have reacted to our shifting attitudes towards them.

The "Us" in my title includes myself. Like everyone else I have derived my impressions of royalty mainly from newspapers, books, radio and television. My rare encounters with the royal family have been so fleeting that they have added little to what I already knew. Nevertheless I have been an observer of royal life for over sixty years and will use my small experiences as typical, and add to them my family's.

My father wrote the official life of King George V. He was commissioned to write it by an old friend, Sir Alan Lascelles, George VI's private secretary, who warned him, "You must always remember, Harold, that you will not be writing an ordinary biography. You will be writing mythology, and the myth is one of gossamer fragility. Nothing discreditable about the monarchy, nothing uncouth, nothing comic must enter your book."

"But what if I discover that the King acted from time to time foolishly or ignominiously?"

"You must leave it out."

My father undertook the task with some misgivings, and by concentrating more on the reign than on the Monarch, emerged with credit and a knighthood.

Until recently the Monarch, and those closest to the throne, have been given the benefit of the doubt. The deference due to them in life was sustained after death. So majestic, in its literal and figurative sense, was the royal role, that by common consent the Monarch was endowed with superlative qualities which astonished even the Monarch in person. An example is Queen Victoria's Diamond Jubilee. The people, almost unanimously, declared that they loved her, when she was unlovable, ugly, disagreeable and remote. People's capacity for self-delusion was one of her chief assets. They were not loving her, but what she stood for, Britain's glory and success. They did not want to hear bad things about her, nor about her two successors. In the 1900s it was inconceivable that a courtier should make public the fact that when Edward VII lay dying, both his wife and his mistress were present at his deathbed, one each side. Today we are less inhibited. Private lives, even royal lives, have become matters not just for gossip but for publication. My father, in 1948, was shackled by the old conventions.

George V was a virtuous man, and Queen Mary virtuous to the point of rigidity. "No member of our family", she once said, "should smile in public." My father was dismayed to discover, as soon as he began to examine the archives at Windsor, that excellent as King George was as King, he was a very dull man. In his lifetime, and after his death, he was represented as wise, statesmanlike and infinitely kind. But King George was not a kind man, even to his children. He expected them to treat him not as their father, but as the King. He was so unsympathetic to his second son's stammer ("Get it out!" he would shout at him) that it made the stammer worse. Owen Morshead, the King's librarian, once told my father, "The House of Windsor produces bad parents. Like ducks, they trample on their young." Nor was the King in any true sense a statesman. He had a loathing for change. He had no understanding of new ideas like socialism or women's rights. His elder son wrote that he "disapproved of Soviet Russia, painted fingernails, women who smoked in public, cocktails, frivolous hats, American jazz and the growing habit of going away for weekends". Obliged by his position to associate with clever people, he disliked them for their cleverness. In his published correspondence one can detect his irritability, which was natural in a man who enjoyed the highest status but no power. Like his grandmother, he was astonished by the people's rapturous acclaim at his 1935 Jubilee. "I'd no idea that they felt like that about me," he said rather touchingly on returning from an East End tour. "I'm beginning to think that they must really like me for myself." When he died the next year, he was profoundly mourned. Bloomsbury was not so generous. "The British public has had a fit of grief which surpasses all ever known," Virginia Woolf wrote to her nephew. "It is a curious survival of barbarism, emotionalism, heraldry, ecclesiasticism, sheer sentimentality, snobbery, and some feeling for the very commonplace man who was so like ourselves."

The most that could be said of his reign was delicately put by James Pope-Hennessy in his official life of Queen Mary: "It witnessed violent social and other upheavals. Throughout all these, the monarchy remained stable, safe and an example of old-fashioned rectitude and simplicity." My father took the same line. If the King was not clever, he had common sense. If he was conservative, it is the duty of the Monarch to apply the brakes when his Ministers are treading too firmly on the accelerator. If he was sometimes sharp in private, he could also be gentle. One of the attractive sides of his character was his fondness for his grandchildren. It was he who gave Princess Elizabeth the affectionate sobriquet Lilibet. But he was a lazy man, politically and socially. He hated entertaining and being entertained, dining alone with Queen Mary night after night except for liveried footmen standing behind their chairs, immobile and dumb. The Duke of Windsor told my father, "His hatred of being bothered was almost pathological. He had a wonderful capacity for avoiding business." If, in writing the biography of such a man, you are forbidden even to hint at his weaknesses, he becomes unreal. "For seventeen years before his accession," my father wrote to my mother, "he did nothing at all but kill animals and stick in stamps," and in the privacy of his diary he wrote, "If my theme is to be a simple man who did his duty, how can I justify the fact that he made no effort at all to prepare himself for the throne? One cannot write a long book solely on the theme of rectitude." But he did. On reading the proofs, Queen Mary asked him to omit only two phrases, one from a letter of Queen Alexandra calling the Kaiser "That ass William",

4

and the other from her husband's tutor, starting "My darling little Georgy", which she thought inappropriate for the future King.

George VI inherited from his father his rectitude and conservatism, and Elizabeth II has inherited the same virtues from her father. Between them came a king who renounced both. Princess Elizabeth did not know her uncle well. She was only ten years old when he abdicated, and nieces are rarely privileged to hear about their uncles' peccadilloes. But his extraordinary fate had a strong influence on her concept of monarchy. She would be his opposite, in destiny and conduct.

It is difficult to exaggerate Edward's popularity as Prince of Wales. He was handsome, pleasing, active, brave. Young women loved him with a distant hopelessness, humming to themselves, "I danced with a man who danced with a girl who danced with the Prince of Wales." His qualities perfectly matched his youthful role. He was no intellectual. His recreations were hunting, skiing, point-to-points and flirtation. He had been courageous in the First World War, and to his credit was embarrassed by the award of the Military Cross because he had not won it in the front line. On his official tours abroad he behaved exactly as people wanted a prince to behave. He was gallant, audacious, innovative, charming to the women and polite to the men. He could pretend a serious interest in Anglo-Argentinian trade, and at a Canadian rodeo mount a bucking bronco. At home his politics were right-wing to the extent of showing sympathy with Oswald Mosley's New Party (a fact which Mosley asked me to suppress from my father's published diaries) but the public neither knew nor cared about his political opinions. He was Prince Charming and would make a wonderful king.

That was his public image. Those who worked for him took a different view. In 1927, during the Canadian tour,

Alan Lascelles wrote to a colleague, "It would be a real dis-aster if, by any ill chance, he was called to accede to the throne now, and I see no prospect of his fitting himself any better." What were his complaints? The Prince's head was not turned by adulation. He loathed it. But he considered that his private life was quite separate from the public show, without realising that the private life of someone in his position and with his vitality generates greater fascina-tion than his public performance. Soon after the Abdication, Lascelles spoke to my father about this early period: "He had no spiritual or aesthetic side at all. When I was in America with him, he was so debauched and drunken that I had to resign. At parties he ignored the wives of the grandees to dance with the prettiest girls ... He really loathed being King, and was determined to get out of it as soon as he could."

When George V died, his son was horrified by the responsibilities thrust upon him. The public's acclaim depressed him. He would be expected, constantly, to act out of character, and to perform dignified roles that bored him excessively. He was not seriously interested in politics. In retrospect he made the solemn declaration, "My modest ambition was to broaden the base of the monarchy ... to make it a little more responsive to the changed circum-stances of my times," but he had no idea what he meant by that, except that he wanted a less stuffy Court where he could enjoy himself. He had no ambition to upset the existing hierarchy. His only innovations were to establish the King's Flight within the RAF (he was the first British Monarch to fly), and to waive the rule that the Yeomen of the Guard must wear beards. His later conduct as Governor-General of the Bahamas showed that he was capable of applying himself to dull routine, but as King he showed his detestation of it. He avoided duty meetings whenever he could and left State documents unread. He upset his staff by cutting their salaries in a manic burst of economy for which there was no need and no public demand.

Then came Mrs Simpson. When her character became known, it was thought astonishing that the King, who could have chosen any woman in the world as his Queen, should be enraptured by so plain and charmless an adventuress. Philip Ziegler, his biographer, called her, "harsh, dominating, often abominably rude. She treated the Prince at the best like a child who needed keeping in order, at the worst with contempt. He invited it, and begged for more." His infatuation gave him perverse strength. When Ernest Simpson, before their divorce, asked him directly what his intentions were, he replied, "Do you really think that I would be crowned without Wallis at my side?" Society was puzzled. Something of their uncertainty is shown by an entry in my father's diary of 2 April 1936:

I dine with Mrs Simpson to meet the King. Black tie; black waistcoat; taxi to Bryanston Court. An apartment dwelling; a lift; butler and maid at door; drawing-room; many orchids and white arums. The guests consist of Lady Oxford, Lady Cunard, Lady Colefax, Kenneth Lindsay, the Counsellor of the US Embassy in Buenos Aires plus wife, Alexander Woollcott. Ernest Simpson enters, bringing in the King. We all bow and curtsey. The King looks well and gay. He passes brightly from group to group... Something snobbish in me is rather saddened by all this. Mrs Simpson is a perfectly harmless type of American, but the whole setting is slightly second-rate. I do not wonder that the Sutherlands and Stanleys are sniffy about it all.

By October his view had hardened. "It irritates me that that silly little man should destroy a great Monarchy by giggling into a flirtation with a third-rate American."

The news of the King's intention did not gradually seep into the public's consciousness. It exploded. The drama lasted only a week, 3–10 December 1936. Stanley Baldwin had judged the people's reactions correctly. The working class, more royalist than the King, were firmly opposed to his marriage, not so much because of his inadequacy as for her unworthiness as a twice-divorced American whose love for the King was in doubt, but not her ambition. A mistress was tolerable for a king, but if she becomes his wife, she will not do as queen. After announcing the Abdication, Baldwin left the Chamber of the House of Commons, and bumped into my father. "The man is mad," he said. "MAD. He could see nothing but that woman. He lacks religion. I told his mother so. I love the man. But he must go."

For the remainder of their lives the Windsors were more of an embarrassment to the monarchy than a menace. None of the royal family attended their wedding, and the Duchess, to her fury, was denied the title of Royal Highness. The abiding lesson of the crisis was that the people do not want a maverick Monarch, and that in the last resort he can be dismissed by Parliament, in spite of the oath to which all MPs subscribe on first taking their seats: "I swear by Almighty God that I will be faithful and bear true allegiance to His/Her Majesty, according to law. So help me God." The monarchy itself was not under threat because the law of succession threw up a man whose temperament was in total contrast to his brother's – Albert, who took the name of George VI.

## II

KING George's disadvantages were many. He had not expected the job, and did not want it. On the eve of his accession he said to Mountbatten, "Dickie, this is absolutely terrible. I am quite unprepared for it. David has been trained for this all his life. I've never even seen a State paper. I'm only a naval officer. It's the only thing I know about." To his mother he confessed not only anxiety, but despair. She told my father, when he visited her at Marlborough House in 1949, "He sobbed on my shoulder for a whole hour — there, upon that sofa." He did not look like a king. He did not feel like one. To be a memorable king, one must enjoy being a king, and he regarded the prospect with dread. He was shy and hesitant, and his lack of self-confidence was exaggerated by his stammer. Old films show him turning away glumly from a stranger, while the Queen would linger, interested in what the man had to say. Chips Channon, who knew the King well, made this comment after his death:

He was uninteresting and unintellectual, but doubtless well-meaning. He improved with the years. His natural shyness and inferiority complex towards his elder brother made him on the defensive. He had no wit, no learning, no humour except of rather a schoolboy brand. He was nervous, ill at ease, though slightly better after some champagne, and had few interests other than shooting. He had few friends, and was almost entirely dependent on the Queen whom he worshipped.

Those were his drawbacks. But because the public cannot approach royalty closely, we invent for them a character. We saw a man who looked elegant in uniform and tailored suits, who did not shirk his duties, and was obviously determined to overcome his hesitancy, unexciting and unexcitable, English to the core, decent and reliable. Above all, he was not like his brother, nor was his Queen like Wallis Simpson. Indeed, his family was his principal asset. His wife was a woman who had an extraordinary capacity to please, and his daughters were two girls on whom the whole nation beamed. Princess Margaret wrote after his death, "You know what a wonderful person he was. He was the very heart and centre of our family, and nobody could have had a more loving and thoughtful father." Such affection cannot be feigned, even in bereavement, and something of this sentiment was echoed by the common man.

The King's Coronation was a triumph. It signalled a return to normality. As he took up his duties, he gained in confidence. Although his speeches were written for him, a man's diary is his own, and his is firm and sensible. Unlike his father, he was not called upon to make any serious political decisions. He was conservative and distrusted change. He once said to my mother, who told him that Knole, her family home, had passed into the ownership of the National Trust, "Everything is going now. Before long I shall also have to go." Politically he was unadventurous and short-sighted. Like many others he supported Neville Chamberlain's policy of appeasing the Dictators, and appeared with him on the balcony of Buckingham Palace after his return from Munich, which some thought unwise, because the Munich Pact was a matter of high controversy in which the Monarch should not be engaged. In May 1940 he favoured Lord Halifax, not Winston Churchill, as Chamberlain's successor, distrusting Churchill for his flamboyant and unpredictable character, his support for Edward

VIII at the time of the Abdication, and his hostility to Chamberlain. That was soon to change.

The war, and Churchill, made a king of him. As his father had found in the First War, a king, unlike his generals, is elevated by victory, but not diminished by defeat. At first he wondered what his role should be. Wearing the uniform of the highest rank in all three services, he had no power of command. In April 1940 he wrote pathetically in his diary, "Everyone is working at fever heat except me." The deliberate targeting of Buckingham Palace by the Luftwaffe transformed him and the Queen into symbols of resistance, and their tours of east London and other stricken cities made a contribution to national morale that could have been achieved by no other persons in no other way. He was also diligent in visiting troops in their home stations, where his manner was friendly and reassuring. He came to Perth, where my Grenadier battalion was stationed just before we embarked for North Africa, and I remember how tactfully he dealt with an awkward situation. Our Colonel, in a spasm of untypical nervousness, had a lapse of memory in introducing his officers. "May I present my Second-in-Command, sir, Major..." Then silence. "Tufnell," whispered the Adjutant. "And my Adjutant, Captain..." It was dreadful. "Well," the King said gaily, "let's take the rest as read, and go into luncheon." That was the serene side of his nature. He could sympathise.

He went abroad, to Algeria, Tunisia, Italy and France whenever operations quietened down, but such was the tension in the field that his presence was less effective than at home. I saw him drive past a group of soldiers with our Commander-in-Chief, General Alexander, and he did not look the part. He had been in Italy only three days, and was upset by the climate, the food and the rough response of soldiers just out of battle. He was paler than us, a tartan rug spread over his knees to save them from sunburn, and when we raised a cheer, it was not wholehearted, and he did not respond. The notion that soldiers risk their lives for King and Country bears no relation to the truth. They risk them because they do not want to let down their friends.

On the other hand, when the circumstances were right, the King had an extraordinarily emotive appeal. His visit to Malta in 1943 was the high point of his whole reign. The idea was his own. The islanders had survived the fury of German and Italian air attack and were near starvation. In recognition of their courage the King had already conferred on the island his own decoration, the George Cross. Now he wanted to visit it in person. He was advised that the risks were still great, but he was determined. On the night of 19 June he embarked in North Africa on the cruiser *Aurora*. As they approached the Grand Harbour of Valetta at dawn, the news was broadcast to the people, and they crowded the quays and bastions of the ancient fortifications to welcome him. In the bright morning sunlight they saw a slim figure in a white uniform standing alone on an elevated platform at the cruiser's bow. He was as deeply moved by their acclamation as they were by his unexpected presence. There was no pretence about it on either side. It was much the same at the end of the war, when he stood with Churchill on the balcony of Buckingham Palace to salute the crowds. They wanted to see them stand together, the leader and the Monarch, and in cheering them, they were cheering themselves.

In the post-war period the King's reputation was firmly established. There were no minor royals to disgrace him or divert attention from his central role. The Duke of Windsor lived abroad in near obscurity and, of his other brothers, the Duke of Kent had died in an air accident in 1942 and the Duke of Gloucester never achieved, or desired, public notoriety. The royal family carried out their duties, at home and abroad, conscientiously. The King accepted a Labour government with public welcome whatever his private misgivings. His official biographer, John Wheeler-Bennett, wrote, "Mr Attlee's personal relationship with King George was not at first easy. Both were essentially shy men, and the initiation of conversation did not come easily to either of them. At the outset the Prime Minister's audiences were not infrequently marked by long silences." It soon went better. The King particularly enjoyed the company of Aneurin Bevan, Minister of Health. With becoming diffidence, Bevan asked permission to express his long-felt admiration for the way the King had overcome his speech defect. As one who had stammered badly as a boy, he appreciated this achievement in full measure. The King asked him how he liked the responsibilities of a government department after so long in opposition. "He laughed at that," the King recorded in his diary, "I found him easy to talk to." His attitude to socialist reforms and Indian independence was passive, which benefited the government, because if the King makes no protest, there can be nothing much wrong with it.

Life was not always so agreeable. The King was tired by the strain of the war, and some of his duties, political and social, were irksome to him. "Now and again," my father wrote after meeting him, "there is that sullen, heavy-lidded, obstinate dulling of the blue eyes." In 1946 I was ordered by my adjutant (for I was still a serving soldier) to escort the Prime Minister's daughter, Felicity Attlee, to a ball at Buckingham Palace. She hated it. She disapproved of "all this flummery" and could not dance. She was an awkward partner and, to amuse her, I suggested that we explore the Palace. I had noticed that a suite of rooms leading off the ballroom was unlocked and dimly lit, perhaps intended for distinguished guests but now unoccupied. "Let's have a look," I said. I conducted her through the sitting room, the study, two bedrooms and a bathroom.

On returning, we bumped into a figure in the doorway. It was the King, presumably on his way to the lavatory. "What are you doing here?" he snapped angrily.

"I did not know that these rooms were private, Your Majesty."

"Well, they are. Get back at once."

Miss Attlee was in greater distress than me. "He'll tell my father." I assured her that this was most unlikely, as the King had no idea who either of us was. In any case, mine was the responsibility. But she was inconsolable, and we spent another three unhappy hours at the ball because we could not leave before the royal family, who were hugely enjoying themselves, apart from the King himself. I could not blame him. Such parties had ceased to give him any pleasure, and he was unwell, with incipient cancer.

It was on that occasion that I first saw Queen Elizabeth, later the Queen Mother. My father had met her when she was Duchess of York on a visit to Berlin, where he was Counsellor at the British Embassy. He was delighted by her social dexterity. "She has the astonishing gift of being sincerely interested in dull people and dull occasions," he wrote. "She creates a radiance of goodwill." He thought it "a tragedy" that she should be royal, because she would have enjoyed herself much more if she were not, since people did not act naturally in her company. She had an instinct for spotting the shyest person in the room and drawing them into the conversation. She had unusually large eyes, which she opened wide and directed on the person she was talking to, not intimidatingly, but solicitous, genuinely interested in what they had to say. Her tact was legendary. Once in South Africa she was accosted by a tough Boer politician who replied to her compliment on the beauty of his country, "The country's all right. It's the English I can't stand."

"I sympathise entirely," she said in her most Scottish

accent. "You see, I married one. But you soon get used to them."

She invented the royal walkabout, the smile, the wave. She found instinctively the middle ground between Queen Mary's aloofness and the matiness of Continental royals. She embodied the traditional values of her race. Astonishingly, she was the first Queen of England since Catherine Parr to be born British. No royal person understood better than she did what ordinary people were like, because she was at heart an ordinary person, less grand than many of her ladies-in-waiting. She was amusing and amused. A *Times* leader said of her, "She would lay a foundation stone as though she had discovered a new and delightful way of spending an afternoon," and if something went wrong with the arrangements, it made her day. Once she lunched with my parents at Sissinghurst, for she had a great love of gardens, and the soufflé flopped. She was not in the least disturbed. She insisted on consoling our cook, telling her that she had never managed to make soufflés stand up straight. We knew very well that she had never attempted it in her life. She was something of an actress, as all royals have to be.

This was the woman who sustained the King for many years, and set a new standard, a new manner, for royalty. After lunching with her in July 1940, my father wrote in his diary, "She told me that she is being instructed every morning how to fire a revolver. I expressed surprise. 'Yes,' she said, 'I shall not go down like the others.'" He wondered afterwards whom she could have meant by "the others", and decided she must be referring to the foreign royalties, like the Belgians, Bulgars and Yugoslavs, who had succumbed tamely to Hitler. When in 1966 I came across this passage in my father's diaries, I thought it best to ask permission before publishing it. The Queen Mother's Private Secretary replied that she had no objection, since it was true. But what was the purpose of all this practising unless she intended to use her revolver against a foreign invader? I imagined the scene. The Germans land in Britain. They succeed in capturing London. The *Wehrmacht* General sends an SS lieutenant to seize the Palace, which the Führer intends to use as his headquarters. A few shots are fired in the forecourt, but resistance is soon overcome, and the young officer mounts the staircase to the private apartments. He opens the drawing-room door. The Queen is there. He salutes. She raises her revolver, and ... But does she? Years later I sat next to her at a lunch party, and reminded her of her revolver practice. She well remembered it. But I did not dare put to her the question in my mind.

# III

WHEN the King died unexpectedly on 6 February 1952 he left his wife as Queen Mother and his elder daughter as Queen. Edward Ford, his Secretary, brought the "bad news" to Churchill early in the morning, when the Prime Minister was still in bed. "It is not just bad news," he said. "It is the worst." A little later he added, "I do not know the new Queen. She is but a child." She was not a child. She was twenty-five years old, married with two children, and with considerable experience behind her. After Shirley Temple, the actress, she was the most famous young woman in the world.

It happened that on the very day of the King's death, there was a by-election in Bournemouth, at which I was the Conservative candidate. The news reached us at eleven in the morning of polling day. My agent met me with a solemn face: "The King is dead." We were stunned. Would the voters think it improper to cast a vote with the King not yet cold in his bed? Would they assume that the election was cancelled? My mother, who had come to support me that day, took charge. She telephoned to friends at the BBC and asked them to announce on the one o'clock news that the poll would go ahead. Then we patrolled the streets with loudspeakers proclaiming that Bournemouth had the honour of electing the first MP in the reign of Queen Elizabeth II. They elected me. "How furious the great Elizabeth would be", my father wrote in his diary, "to know that she has been succeeded by this sweet girl."

The Queen did not hear the news until half an hour after all Britain knew it. She was in a remote part of Kenya, where communications were difficult, and she had spent the night up a fig tree which overlooked a pool where elephants and baboons came to drink and be photographed. She was on the first leg of an Empire tour, which was immediately cancelled, and she flew back to London to be greeted at the airport by Winston Churchill and his Cabinet. Everyone has seen the photograph taken of her, one of the most touching in her reign, as she descended the aircraft steps, so young and so very much alone.

What was known of her character and fitness to reign? I must go back several years to outline her early life, and how she was prepared for her immense task.

Princess Elizabeth was born on 21 April 1926, and her sister Margaret four years later. Their upbringing, described at the time as "normal" for children of their class, was anything but normal. Elizabeth made the cover of *Time* magazine at the age of three, and the first biography of her was published when she was four. The girls never went to school because their father feared that they might meet "wrong types". They lived in a London house, 145 Piccadilly, which had twenty-five bedrooms and was staffed by sixteen servants. For holidays they went to Sandringham, Glamis (their mother's family home) and Balmoral. For friends there were the few aristocratic girls who were allowed to join the Buckingham Palace Company of Girl Guides and were expected to curtsey to the Princesses on first meeting them. Until the outbreak of war, they met no boys.

If this sounds constrictive, it was in fact a happy, uninhibited childhood. While the girls were denied the experience of most children, they were spared many of its traumas. There was no shortage of money, no competition, no bullying, no parental discord, no domestic troubles, and they met interesting people who treated them with gentle curiosity. The notion that they were royal was not a sudden revelation to them. They became accustomed to it from their earliest years, and had privileged places on the most glamorous occasions, like their grandfather's Jubilee and their father's Coronation. These events were highly enjoyable, and they were spared the tedium. Everything was done for them. They had few worries.

Although the Princesses shared these experiences and were devoted to each other, they developed differently. Elizabeth, long before she realised that she would succeed her father on the throne, was calm, sensible, serious, with a love of neatness and order. Churchill, observing her at Balmoral when she was only two, commented to his wife, "She is a character. She has an air of authority and reflectiveness astonishing in an infant," and it is equally astonishing that a Prime Minister who did not like infants should notice it. Her father realised that she was "the best of the two". But he loved Margaret more. Mark Bonham-Carter, who knew both sisters well when they were teenagers, said that King George seemed amazed that he could have fathered so glittering a child. Margaret was born with a talent to amuse. She danced, she mimicked, she played the piano, she was high-spirited and loved all things bright and beautiful, of which she was herself the perfect example, in manner and person. Together the two girls were what Ben Pimlott has called, "a distillation of British wholesomeness".

They were barely educated. For the first twelve years after infancy their only teacher was Marion Crawford ("Crawfie"), a Scottish working-class girl whose only training had been in an Edinburgh academy, to which she intended to return as a child psychologist. The Queen had engaged her as a temporary governess. She remained for sixteen years, much respected, much loved. While not a strict disciplinarian, she was excellent at nursery and schoolroom lore, adventurous, strong, funny. After a fashion, she taught the girls English, French and history, but only for seven hours a week. For a time there was also a French governess, and Elizabeth was given instruction on the Constitution by the Provost of Eton. Crawfie was uninterested in culture. Surrounded by the greatest art collection still in private hands, the children were never encouraged to look at it. My brother Benedict, who was Deputy Surveyor of the King's Pictures at the time, was not once invited to guide their taste.

But Crawfie had wider ambitions for the girls, taking them on educational trips and even on the London Underground. To her dismay, she is best remembered for her "betrayal" of the royal family three years after leaving their service. She published, first in a magazine, then in a book, an account of her charges called *The Little Princesses*. There was nothing in it that today would be regarded as indiscreet or offensive, nothing more revealing than what several ex-courtiers have let slip, with impunity, about the Queen's adult life. Crawfie provided biographers with invaluable details about their hidden childhood, sentimental in part, recording the funny things that children say, their nursery games, their love of dogs and ponies. It seemed to their parents unforgivable to reveal such trivia to the world, and Crawfie was never forgiven. That she wrote the book for money was in their eyes the most scandalous aspect of the affair, for it would encourage other royal employees to do the same. It did permanent damage to relations between Buckingham Palace and the Press.

The Crawfie years covered the whole period of the Second World War. There was no question of sending the Princesses to Canada for the duration, like many other children of wealthy families. The Queen put it simply and effectively: "They would not leave without me, and I would not leave without the King, and the King would never leave." She might have chosen for her children some remote refuge in the country, which would not be divulged to the Press, but she chose Windsor Castle. There could scarcely be a more prominent target for German bombers, but it escaped unscathed, unlike Buckingham Palace, which was hit nine times. There was the continuing problem whether to bring up the Princesses "normally", mixing them with their contemporaries in simple circumstances, or to guard them from kidnap by security men and from undesirables by courtiers. The decision was to protect them. The publicity line was that they were living austerely, subject to the same disciplines and rationing as everyone else. The possibility that they might go to a university was never considered, and the occasional party and theatricals at the Castle were attended only by the daughters of the staff and young officers of the Grenadier Guards whose training battalion was stationed at Windsor Barracks. In 1942, on her sixteenth birthday, Princess Elizabeth was appointed Colonel of the Regiment, and as her first public duty inspected the battalion in the Castle's courtyard.

Later, she toured the Welsh coalfields with her parents and launched the battleship HMS *Vanguard* on the Clyde. Looking back, it might be said that her wartime youth was too confined. Her acquaintance could have been widened, and she could have played an earlier and more prominent part in the war effort. As it was, she first put on uniform in the closing months of the war when she joined the Women's Auxiliary Territorial Service (ATS) at Aldershot, where she learnt how to drive and maintain army vehicles, but at lectures she was seated apart from the other girls, and returned each night to sleep at the Castle. On VE night she was permitted, for the first time, to mingle with the crowds. She and her sister, escorted by a young officer, walked unrecognised down the Mall and through Piccadilly, and stood outside the Palace calling for their parents to show themselves once more on the balcony. "Poor darlings," the King wrote in his diary that night, "they have never yet had any fun."

It is true that they had never enjoyed country house parties, nightclubs, illicit escapades or eccentric behaviour, but Elizabeth did not desire that sort of life, and Margaret, who did, managed to create for herself a fantasy world within the palaces and increasingly outside them. Elizabeth accepted that for the rest of her life she would be told, or at least advised, what to do and say in public. Jock Colville, who had been Churchill's Secretary and now became hers, wrote, "She has the sweetest of characters, but she is not easy to talk to … Her worth, which I take to be very real, is not on the surface." But she was not unresponsive. She did not seem to mind the ogling stares and intrusive cameras that plagued her public appearances, and her head was never turned by adulation. Film made of her at the time shows a girl of charming but not startling good looks, never morose and never flamboyant, well-mannered, eager, alert. She was not indifferent to the outer world, nor ignorant of its travails. Among her Grenadier companions were men who had suffered terribly in the war. One of them was Mark Bonham-Carter, who had survived a ferocious battle in Tunisia, and escaped from a German prison camp. She wanted to hear from him what he had endured.

Her most significant experience in the immediate post-war years was her visit to South Africa in 1947. It was her first journey abroad, and her first direct contact with the Empire. When the family embarked at Portsmouth on HMS *Vanguard*, Britain was experiencing the harshest winter on record, aggravated by a shortage of household fuel. The King wondered whether it was his duty to cancel the tour, which might seem heartless to his shivering people, but he was dissuaded by Attlee, who pointed out that a cancellation might give the impression that the crisis was more serious than it actually was. To ease the King's conscience, the first half of the three-week voyage was spoiled by violent storms, and the whole family was endlessly seasick. Having crossed the Equator, they met with balmy weather, and in the sunshine the Princesses played deck games with the young naval officers and equerries, one of whom was the handsome Group Captain Peter Townsend. The film of their frolics on board shows the two girls uninhibited by watching parents and senior officers. It was an adventure they were determined to enjoy.

On arrival at Cape Town they were greeted by Field Marshal Smuts, Prime Minister of the Union, whose motive in inviting them was not only personal, but highly political. South Africa was split between black and white, and between the two white races, of English and Dutch descent, who were about to engage in an election which would determine South Africa's future relations with the Crown. Smuts believed that the tour would swing public opinion to the royalist side against the Nationalists under Herzog. Princess Elizabeth would be his trump card. Her youth, her vivacity, the tantalising but unconfirmed rumour that she was engaged to Philip Mountbatten and the knowledge that she would one day be Queen would win all hearts and votes.

Many of the King's duties were ceremonial – the opening of Parliament, the parade of troops, the dedication of battleships and dams, the obligatory visit to the grave of Cecil Rhodes – but there were social functions too, some on a grand scale (banquets, balls), some more humble ("Please, Your Majesty, stay for another five minutes, for the fourth form – they have practised their dance so many times, and would be terribly disappointed.") The three women in the party stood this better than the King, who was irritated by the Security – he called them the Gestapo –

impatient with the protocol and infuriated by the Nationalists, who were sometimes openly hostile to the visitors. "I'd like to shoot them all," he muttered to the Queen. ("But, Bertie, you can't shoot them *all!*") There were many consolations – the climate, the opulence of their accommodation and the food compared with the privations of the last eight years in Britain, and above all the beautiful white train which was their home for thirty-five nights as it snaked through the mountains and the veld as far north as Southern Rhodesia.

Elizabeth normally had no role except to walk behind her parents and be worshipped by the crowds ("Stay with us!" "Leave her behind!") but she had a few solo functions like declaring open a graving dock in East London. Her big moment came on her twenty-first birthday. A ball was held in her honour, at which Smuts gave her a diamond neck-lace and the key to Cape Town. The culmination was her broadcast to the youth of the Empire, how it had "saved the world, and now had to save itself". Then her mood changed, and with a vibrant voice, she declared,

There is a motto which has been borne by many of my ancestors – a noble motto – "I serve." I cannot quite do as they did, but through the inventions of science I can do what was not possible for any of them. I can make my solemn act of dedication with a whole Empire listening. I should like to make that dedication now. It is very simple. I declare before you that my whole life, whether it be long or short, shall be devoted to your service and the service of our great Imperial family, but I shall not have the strength to carry out this resolution unless you join with me, as I now invite you to do.

It was a declaration based upon a false premise, that the Empire was likely to endure, when it was in the first stages of disintegration. The South African election ousted the Smuts government for one which imposed apartheid on the country. Nor was it evident in what way the youth of the Empire could "join" with her in her high ambition. It did not matter. There was a purity about her broadcast, like an oath of allegiance. She had not composed it herself. It was written by the King's Secretary, Sir Alan Lascelles. Years later he told my father that when she had read through the draft, he asked her, "Can you say this?"

"Yes, I can."

"Do you sincerely believe it?"

"Yes, I do."

In his biography of the Queen, Ben Pimlott quotes a letter which Sir Alan wrote to his wife on their way home:

From the inside, the most satisfactory feature of the whole business is the remarkable development of P'cess E. She has got all P'cess Mary's solid and endearing qualities plus a perfectly natural power of enjoying herself…Not a great sense of humour, but a healthy sense of fun. Moreover, when necessary, she can take on the old bores with much of her mother's skill, and never spares herself in that exhausting part of royal duty. For a child of her years, she has astonishing solicitude for other people's comfort; such unselfishness is not a normal characteristic of that family.

Those were prescient words. Add to them her competence, her love of order and punctuality, and a certain decorum, and you have the present Queen.

On their return, the first question in everyone's mind was her engagement. Philip, it appears, was not a demonstrative lover, and at first there was some doubt about his dedication to her. He was young, carefree, ambitious for his naval career in which he had already distinguished himself, and reluctant, it was thought by some, to engage himself for life to a role where he would be shackled by convention and subordinate to his wife. Her unwavering devotion decided him. Their engagement was first announced in Athens, his parental city, on 8 July 1947, a day before it was confirmed by the Palace. The Princess attended a ball that night at Apsley House, without her fiancé, and I was one of the Grenadier officers whom she invited to dance with her, as I had written the wartime history of the Regiment, of which she was Colonel, and had been given permission to dedicate the book to her. We talked, but no mention of her engagement was yet possible. "I fear I do not dance very well," I said.

"Nor do I," she replied untruthfully, "because I was never allowed to ski. All skiers are beautiful dancers."

That is all I remember of our conversation. What I do remember is that it was one of the most magical evenings of my life.

Philip's youth had been extraordinarily varied. He was born Greek, but could not speak it. His mother was Mountbatten's sister. His grandfather and uncle were both Kings of Greece. When he was only eighteen months old, his father was driven into exile by the revolutionary faction, and he settled in impoverishment at St Cloud, near Paris. His parents separated, his mother becoming a religious recluse, his father moving to Monte Carlo, where he died in 1944. Philip was sent to school at Cheam in Surrey and then to Gordonstoun. Although technically a foreigner, he was quintessentially British. In the war he distinguished himself in the Royal Navy in the Mediterranean and the Pacific, and seemed destined for high command. Then Princess Elizabeth fell in love with him. There were some objections to their marrying. Crawfie thought Elizabeth too young to marry, and Philip unpolished, too forthright. It was rumoured that the King and Queen also had their doubts. A courtier told my father that they thought Philip "ill-tempered, uneducated, and would probably not be faithful", and it did not help that he was penniless, and that his four sisters had all married Germans.

English xenophobia was sublimated into delight for so handsome a couple, and as the wedding approached, vicarious love for them reached a crescendo of sentimentality. Mountbatten, who was credited with encouraging his nephew's suit, looked more like a father than an uncle, and Philip more like a future King than the consort of a future Queen. He was naturalised British, and created Duke of Edinburgh. The wedding took place in Westminster Abbey on 20 November 1947. It was not a modest affair: 350 girls had worked on the bride's wedding dress for seven weeks, sewing on 10,000 costume pearls. It had a political effect too, in committing the Labour Party to the monarchy, and showing the world that a Socialist government could stage a glamorous event, without apology, in the midst of an economic blizzard. But having watched the ceremony on television, I wrote in my diary, "When Winston came in, everyone stood up and bowed. When Attlee came in, nobody noticed that he had even arrived." G. M. Trevelyan wrote more graciously, "Affection for a King's person and family adds warmth and drama to every man's rational awareness of his country's political unity and historic tradition. It is a kind of popular poetry in these prosaic times."

They were too good an advertisement for their country to be kept at home. In the spring of 1948 they paid an official visit to Paris, which was as triumphant as President Kennedy's in 1961, and for much the same reason, the glamour of the bride. Jacqueline and Elizabeth were fluent in French, and both in private and public the city acclaimed them. It was known to few people that the Princess was three months pregnant and feeling dreadfully sick. Versailles, Fontainebleau, Vaux-le-Vicomte, a race meeting, a night club were all fitted into four days of the hottest Whitsun anyone could remember. Even de Gaulle was touched. He said that the only people in Britain who were nice to him were the royal family.

Prince Charles was born on 14 November 1948, and Princess Anne in August 1950. During those years the King's health slowly deteriorated. Some of his duties, like Trooping the Colour, were taken by his daughter, and she began to learn her way around Cabinet papers. For some years Philip remained a serving naval officer, and Elizabeth joined him in Malta, where she was able to enjoy a more normal life with his brother officers and Mountbatten, now Commander-in-Chief of the Mediterranean fleet.

In the autumn of 1951 they undertook an arduous tour of Canada, visiting every province by train. In Ottawa they were the guests of the Governor General, Field Marshal Alexander of Tunis. He arranged for them a barn dance for eighty young people, and when Elizabeth protested that she did not have the right clothes, he kitted her out in a short blue skirt and checkered blouse. She enjoyed such occasions. In public, she was less sure of herself. Sarah Bradford has written, "She would sometimes still feel outshone by her confident, glamorous husband, and aware of his effect on the female section of the public. When she attended women's functions without him, she would confide, 'I know they would rather see Philip.'"

They slipped over the border into the United States, to be welcomed at the White House by President Truman. "He fell in love with her," said Martin Charteris, her Secretary. The President told a gathering in the Rose Garden, "We have had many distinguished visitors to this city, but never before have we had such a wonderful couple, who have completely captivated the hearts of all of us." Then he added, in words that became sickly famous,

"When I was a little boy, I read about a fairy princess, and there she is." There is an advantage in greeting guests young enough to be your children. You can adopt a paternal, non-deferential manner. By this time the Princess was becoming accustomed to such hyperbole, and enjoyed doing what she knew she could do best, pleasing strangers by her presence and her youth.

When her father died, the question immediately arose what title she should bear. She had long known that she would be Queen Elizabeth II, but Queen of what? Ireland posed a problem. She was only Queen of part of it. The title was amended to the complex formula which has never ceased to puzzle foreigners: "Queen of the United Kingdom of Great Britain and Northern Ireland". The Commonwealth created other difficulties. She was not an empress, and "Defender of the Faith" seemed inappropriate to countries which were not Christian. It was decided to retain her as Queen of Canada, Australia, New Zealand and South Africa, but the lovely phrase "Queen of the British Dominions beyond the Seas" was replaced by "Queen of her other Realms and Territories". To make her status more explicit, she was also named, for the first time, "Head of the Commonwealth", and Queen of all its member States except those that had become Republics. Curiously, there was no mention of the Commonwealth in the Coronation service. The Territories were named separately, and she as their Sovereign.

The Coronation, on 2 June 1953, was the most solemn moment of her life, surpassing even her wedding and the funerals of her father and mother, fifty years apart. Sixteen months had passed since her accession. It was like a long engagement, and the Coronation a wedding. People had come to love her, and to look ahead to her reign as a new Elizabethan age. The Coronation also marked the end of wartime austerity. Winston Churchill took it on himself against the advice of his experts to end the rationing of sweets and chocolates. People were encouraged to rejoice. A banquet in Westminster Hall, a ball at Hampton Court, were both attended by the Queen. A tented camp for Commonwealth soldiers was pitched in Hyde Park. Flagposts, floral arches, stands for spectators were erected the length of the Mall and Whitehall. Everything was ready for the day. God might have blessed it with sunshine, but delivered a steady drizzle instead. The waiting crowds were drenched, but cheered by anticipation and by the news that spread early in the morning that Edmund Hillary and Sherpa Tenzing had reached the summit of Everest, which seemed, in some mysterious way, symbolic of a nation that had recovered its greatness and its pride.

As the Queen gazed from her window down the Mall, she must have thought how strange it was that these thousands of people had come to honour her alone. She was not just the centre of attention, but its only purpose. Lords and Commons, foreign royalties and ambassadors, were assembling in the Abbey to witness her crowning. Coronations had been held there since William the Conqueror. Hers was the twenty-eighth in a long line. All the accoutrements, part religious, part military, part purely decorative, were recovered from the vaults or designed for the occasion. The nation's leading men and women were all present, except the Duke of Windsor, whose attendance at what might have been *his* Coronation was too embarrassing to contemplate. It was Elizabeth's day, and she enjoyed the drama, just as Archbishop Fisher enjoyed his role as producer and presenter.

She processed down the Mall in the heavy coach drawn by four pairs of Windsor Greys, Prince Philip, dressed as an admiral, sitting beside her. The service lasted three hours. It had been suggested to her that the strain might be too great, and she might welcome an interval of rest. "Not at all," she replied, "I am as strong as a horse. Let it proceed uninterrupted." So it did. Every moment was recorded on television, except the most solemn, the anointing and Communion. At first she had objected to the cameras being admitted to the Abbey, because they might detract from the solemnity of the occasion, blind her by the glare of the arc lights, and broadcast every small error that might occur, as when at her father's Coronation the Archbishop had placed the crown on his head the wrong way round. Every twitch of uncertainty or weariness on her face would be instantly apparent, not to the few thousands in the body of the church, but to the millions outside and to posterity for ever. Then she was persuaded by public demand to change her mind. She only stipulated that her face would not be shown in close-up, a rule which was broken once, without reprimand, when she walked back down the nave after her crowning, confident and serene.

Her fragility and innocence when she sat for the anointing, dressed only in a simple white shift, lent to the ceremony an almost sacrificial quality, as when Joan of Arc stood in Reims Cathedral at the side of Charles whom she had made King. It was a more solemn moment than her wedding, for then she was supported by Philip, and now she was surrounded by forty elderly men who recited the oaths, handed her the orb, the sceptre, the golden spurs, the swords of Mercy, State and Justice, anointed her and crowned her. Dermot Morrah, the Somerset Herald Extraordinary, who stood near her as the Archbishop anointed her on hands, breast and brow, later spoke of "the sense of spiritual exaltation that radiated from her". The crowds outside, listening to the service on loudspeakers, never forgot the hush that descended at that moment. It was as if they were attending a vast memorial mass.

Beautiful archaic words accompanied the slow gestures of the participants. "Sirs," said the Archbishop, "I present to you Queen Elizabeth, your undoubted Queen," at which a hundred Westminster schoolboys shouted, "Vivat! Vivat!" a resonant acclamation, wonderful to cry aloud. When Philip came forward, the first of the peers, to swear allegiance, he spoke these words, "I, Philip, Duke of Edinburgh, do become your liegeman of life and limb, and of earthly worship, and faith and truth will I bear unto you, to live and die, against all manner of folks. So help me God." As the Archbishop anointed her, he invoked ancient Hebraic rituals, "As Solomon was anointed King by Zadok the Priest and Nathan the Prophet, so be thou anointed, blessed and consecrated Queen over the peoples whom the Lord thy God hath given thee to rule and govern."

I was watching the ceremony on television in the House of Commons, where a room had been set aside for MPs not senior enough to be admitted to the Abbey. The medievalism of the service was too much for some left-wing Republicans like Reginald Paget. He guffawed. He found it incredible that any husband could thus address his wife, or that an Anglican priest could utter anachronisms that bore no relevance to the act he was performing. But even Paget succumbed to the excitement of the processions that followed the service. The royal coach was drawn seven miles through the streets of central London, followed by twenty-three open carriages bearing the most distinguished guests, including Winston Churchill and Queen Salote of Tonga, of whom nobody had heard until that day, but who now became the crowd's favourite, for her enormous girth, her cheerful greetings and her indifference to the rain.

Queen Elizabeth II, the undoubted Queen, showed herself to the crowds six times from the Palace balcony, with her husband, mother, little Charles and Anne, and her six maids of honour. David Eccles, the Minister of Works who had organised the procession, when congratulated on its success, replied, "Ah, but I had a splendid leading lady," a remark which was thought vulgar and theatrical. But in a sense he was justified. It had been the most splendid show of 1953 in any country in the world, and the Queen was its star. When the films were shown in America (flown there hour by hour before television could bridge the ocean), there was an outburst of joy and congratulation. There is nothing in the United States, not even the inauguration of a president, to match it. And in Africa and Asia people danced all night.

# IV

THIS is not a biography of the Queen. That has been written by Elizabeth Longford, Sarah Bradford, Ben Pimlott, Robert Lacey, William Shawcross and several others, to all of whom I am indebted for many facts and some opinions. This book is about the nature of monarchy, our reactions to it and the Monarch's reactions to us. To continue a chronological narrative of the Queen's reign is unnecessary. Instead, I will telescope her middle years and portray her first as a person, and then in her public and political roles, in answer to the two questions: "What is she like?" and "What does she do?"

There is a curious contradiction in our knowledge of the Queen. In one sense she is the best-known person in the country. Her activities are recorded almost every day, sometimes at length, sometimes only in the unread Court Circular. She is frequently the central figure on television and radio, and a new 600-page biography of her is published every five years. In another sense we scarcely know her at all. She never says anything in public that is not anodyne and written by someone else. She never gives interviews. Ex-courtiers have been known to lift a corner of the veil, invariably to her credit, and microphones have eavesdropped on snatches of her conversation in greeting an ambassador or talking to a horse, but always inoffensively. That she can do no wrong is one reason why she remains obscure. Lytton Strachey wrote, "A few faults are indispensable to a really popular monarch... What we need is a book entitled *Queen Victoria, by a Personal Acquaintance Who Dislikes Her.*" No such book will ever be written about Queen Elizabeth. She has no evident blemish. It will not be the same with her successors. It was greatly to their advantage that Prince Charles, aged sixteen, was caught sipping cherry brandy in a Stornoway pub, and that Prince Harry, at the same age, gave an illicit party at Highgrove while his father was away.

The Queen's personality appears to us straightforward, uncomplicated, very British. Her appearance is a great asset. We have been reminded in recent years by the replay of old newsreels how lovely she was as a young woman. The Duke of Wellington, who saw her at her first opening of Parliament, was struck by her "astonishing radiance, her lovely teeth, hair and eyes, and that amazing quality of skin. Then add the wonderful voice and the romance, and you have a deeply moving effect." Her figure was excellent, aided by superlative jewels and clothes. Unlike Margaret Thatcher, her exact contemporary, she owed nothing to sexual allure. It was never mentioned in connection with her, not only for reasons of discretion but because her distinctiveness was a-sexual, *Noli me tangere*, but without hostility. Her greatest public gift was her smile. She was seen to laugh, but only once to cry (at an Armistice celebration in November 2002), to be capable of irritation (specially of unpunctuality), but not of anger. She keeps much in reserve. Was she, as a young woman, shy? If so, shyness can be overcome, and she overcame it, substituting reticence. She was curious about the world from which she was excluded. Elizabeth Longford recalls that she would stare out of the window as she was being painted by Annigoni, wondering aloud what all those people in the Mall were like and what they imagined her to be like. Something of that mood is caught in his famous portrait, her favourite as it is of the public. She wears the robes of the Garter loosely, naturally, like a dressing-gown, and looks ahead with serene determination.

In her later years she has retained this calm. Her latest portrait by Lucian Freud (2002) does an injustice not only to her appearance, but to her character. He has made her cross and domineering, when she is neither. She is Annigoni grown up, considerate, efficient, dutiful and private. To meet her is not like meeting any other celebrity. I once saw a man so overcome by her presence that he curtsied to her instead of bowing, and when he explained to me his odd behaviour he giggled, as if to suggest that it was all good fun, when he was simply remembering his embarrassment. We do not know how to behave in her company, how to handle "Your Majesty" in the third person ("As Your Majesty probably knows…"), what subjects of conversation are permissible, and whether one can interrupt or disagree. Mrs Delaney, an intimate of George III and Queen Charlotte, on introducing the novelist Fanny Burney to the Queen, advised her, "I do beg of you, when the King or Queen speak to you, not to answer in mere monosyllables. The Queen often complains to me of the difficulty with which she can get conversation, as she not only has to start the subject but commonly entirely to support it." It is the same today. Royalty inspires awe, and awe ties the tongue. The Queen's manner loosens it. Many things are happening daily, and have happened in the course of a long life, which are subjects of mutual interest, and while the guest's disparity in rank can never be far from his mind, he grows in confidence under her attentive gaze. "Attentive" is the right word. She encourages more than stimulates. She is not formal. In talking to strangers, she refers to her husband as Philip and her son as Charles. She oils the wheels of conversation to the best of her ability, but for her it cannot be much fun.

She has few close friends beyond the Court, and it is due

to them and their families that she is not restricted to a closed circle. Her Secretaries, like Michael Adeane, Rupert Nevill, Martin Charteris and Edward Ford, were clever men, and ladies-in-waiting like Lady Euston and Susan Hussey were intelligent women. Their wide experience and many outside friendships broadened the social range of the Court. I knew only one of them at all well. He was Patrick Plunket, Master of the Household. Only three years older than the Queen, his charming looks, ease of manner, good humour, knowledge of the world and its absurdities made him her special favourite. He was also a considerable connoisseur, a Trustee of the Wallace Collection and of the National Art Collections Fund, and a great organiser of social functions. He loved parties, added gaiety to formal occasions, and if he saw the Queen looking lonely at a ball, according to Bradford, "he would scoop her up and dance with her". He could say to her without impertinence, "Oh you can't possibly wear that hat!" and she would argue with him about it. He had a happy way with people. Once my brother and I arrived to lunch with him at his Victorian house in Kent, and stood outside gazing at its grim exterior. Patrick came out, and said, "I know exactly what you are saying. You are wondering how Patrick can live in such a horrible house. But come inside." It was beautiful. He had wonderful taste and possessions. When he died of cancer in 1973, aged only fifty-one, the Queen regarded his death, said one of her ladies-in-waiting with only slight hyperbole, as "one of the greatest tragedies of her life". He was the one person outside her family who could talk to her on equal terms.

If she had a fault, it was the narrowness of her interests. When everything, and everyone, is available to you, there is a superfluity of opportunity, and you are spoilt for choice. As James Pope-Hennessy described Queen Mary, but with less reason, Queen Elizabeth's nature is "a charming gravity, alertness, and the hope of being amused". She does not enjoy intellectual talk. She has never enjoyed opera, ballet, or classical concerts. She appreciates her fabulous possessions, but they have always been there, and always will. They are agreeable decorations, like the furniture and bibelots, and excellent subjects for conversation. It is said that she rarely reads a book.

She is a countrywoman. She feels relaxed in country clothes and following country pursuits, gathering a train of corgis — an unattractive breed except to their owner — and watching her horses. Her knowledge of them is more than a hobby. It is an expertise. Her closest friend in racing, Lord Porchester, later Lord Carnarvon, said that she would have made a wonderful trainer, with her profound knowledge of breeding, stabling, and "the way a horse moves". She has won every classic except the Derby. It is a specialist sport and, in spite of its popular appeal, elitist. Thoroughbreds are the aristocrats of their kind and the great racecourses — Ascot, Goodwood, Epsom, Longchamp — are like eighteenth-century parks. Few people have so determinedly developed a childhood interest into a lifelong passion. It adds *gravitas* to her private life. I once saw her by chance at Tours in France, where she went for an equine weekend. I was standing in the little airport when a Caravelle fluttered in with a Union Jack flying from its nose. There were more gendarmes than public to meet her. We watched a large Rolls-Royce being given its final polish and the Royal Standard straightened. It was a decoy, for security. The Queen suddenly appeared from behind the airport buildings in a tiny Austin, and was driven rapidly to the stables. I witnessed a similar scene in Kentucky, again by chance, and there the routine was even more discreet and the security even tighter. Both occasions were so unobtrusive, so seriously, so privately done, that I saw her in a new light, dedicated to the science she had made her own.

Her courage is beyond question. There was the incident in 1981, when a seventeen-year-old boy fired blank shots at her as she rode down the Mall to the Trooping the Colour, and she was unflinching, holding her horse steady. A more notorious incident was when, in the following year, a demented youth, Michael Fagan, managed to penetrate Buckingham Palace deeply enough to stand at her very bedside. He woke her up, and engaged her in conversation about his family. The Queen got out of bed, put on her dressing-gown, pointed to the door and shouted at the intruder to get out, but he didn't. It took two calls on her alarm system to alert the police. She was very angry, but not in the least scared. The episode led to the Home Secretary's offer to resign (refused by Thatcher), and added greatly to the enjoyment of Press and public, who were delighted by her conduct, and by the exceptional glimpse it afforded them into her domestic arrangements.

Whether she is deeply or conventionally religious is something that few people can know about any other person. From her early youth religion was urged upon her. She was to become Defender of the Faith, and the Faith was Protestant. With her parents she weekly attended church. Some stirring of satiety is illustrated by her reply as a child to the Archbishop of Canterbury when he invited her to join him for a walk round Sandringham garden, "With pleasure, but please don't talk to me about God. I know all about him already." And in her diary she wrote of the King's Coronation, "At the end, the service got rather boring, as it was all prayers." One is entitled to assume that religion came to mean more to her in later life. It was a refuge in adversity. The Church was a symbol of stability like the Crown itself, but equally open to change and challenge. Because she was so often the central figure in its ceremonies, she identified herself with it, and it gave her comfort.

The greatest influences in her life were her immediate family – her parents, her sister and her husband. Her upbringing endowed her with a sense of duty, her conservatism, her Britishness. As Queen she behaved much as her father had behaved as King, and she never wished to deviate from his example. She inherited more from him than from her mother, whose style was looser, being born a commoner and more adventurous by nature. When her daughter succeeded to the throne, she was left without a definite role, but she created one, never looking upon herself as a Dowager like Queen Mary, unbending and matriarchal. To her, widowhood was in one sense liberation. She would enjoy herself She would be an inspiration to other widows, entertaining and being entertained, travelling abroad in comfort but without fuss, taking up National Hunt racing with gusto, and carrying out royal functions as if she enjoyed them, as she probably did. Subtly she brought about a change in royal behaviour, but never abandoned her rights. She was still a Queen, and took her privileges for granted. While other members of the family economised in response to public criticism, she never did. She had fifty servants and four houses – Clarence House in London, Royal Lodge at Windsor, Birkhall on the Balmoral estate, and the Castle of Mey in Caithness which she restored, and where she spent a few summer weeks in the year – the less windy weeks – not to speak of Walmer Castle, where she was entitled to live as Warden of the Cinque Ports. She did not find these extravagances excessive, and the public willingly accepted them, for fondness of her, just as they accepted her overdrafts, her gin-based martinis and her thickening appearance. Her manner towards the Queen was exemplary. She never overshadowed her. From the moment of her husband's death, she induced her to precede her on entering a room. She never interfered politically, but in family matters like the drama of Princess Margaret and Peter

Townsend, she remained a guiding force, as she had been in the affair of Wallis Simpson.

The Queen and her sister were devoted. Nobody who saw them laughing and galloping down the Royal Mile at Ascot could have doubted it. But they were different people. What Robert Lacey called "the uneasy blend of grandeur and rebellion" in Margaret was absent in Elizabeth. St John Stevas (Lord St John of Fawsley) called Margaret "the cleverest, most beautiful, most charming woman I have ever known". As that was a radio tribute to her on the day of her death, he can be excused the hyperbole, but no man of sense would attribute these qualities to her unless she possessed them in some degree. I did not find her as beautiful as her sister, but there was no doubt about her intelligence and originality. I once escorted her and Lord Snowdon round Knole, my grandfather's house, and was struck by her knowledge and enthusiasm. She loved the arts and literature, patronised the ballet and theatre, wanted a good time, and had it. When she fell in love with Peter Townsend, it was no idle flirtation, but when he declared his love for her to Sir Alan Lascelles, the old courtier is said to have replied, "You must be mad or bad, or both," and Townsend was exiled to Brussels as an air attaché to the embassy for two years, when they could correspond only by post and telephone. The crisis came in 1955, when their wish to marry became public knowledge. People took sides. There were many things in his favour. He was exceptionally good-looking, a heroic fighter pilot in the Battle of Britain, a favourite equerry of George VI who treated him almost as the son he never had, and passionately in love. Against him was his age, sixteen years older than Margaret, which the public thought too wide a gap for happiness, and the impropriety, as it was then considered, of an equerry marrying the King's daughter. Above all, he was divorced, with two children.

Although he had been the innocent party in the divorce, the idea of the Queen's sister marrying a divorced man was anathema to the Queen Mother, and she showed it. The Queen, torn between love for her sister and her mother's prejudice, attempted a compromise: "It's Margaret's life. She alone must decide." This could not be. As a possible but remote heir to the throne, she was subject to the Act, passed in the reign of George III, which required the assent of Parliament to any royal marriage. The problem was referred to the Prime Minister, Anthony Eden, himself divorced and remarried. His Cabinet determined, under the threat of Lord Salisbury's resignation if it were decided otherwise, to refuse the government's approval. If she married Townsend against their wishes, she would forfeit her royal status and Civil List allowance. She would live, probably abroad, as Mrs Peter Townsend, on his exiguous salary. At Balmoral she wrote to herself this stark alternative: "Reasons why I shouldn't marry Peter: because it does harm to the Queen. Reasons why I should marry him: because I couldn't live without him."

In the end it was duty, the Queen Mother's pressure and the prospect of a bleak future that won the day. When she told Archbishop Fisher of her decision to renounce her lover, he raised his hands to bless her, saying, "What a wonderful person the Holy Spirit is!" She gave weight to its mysterious presence in her public announcement. She would not marry Peter Townsend, "mindful of the Church's teaching that Christian marriage is indissoluble". At the time, the country was strongly on Margaret's side. The *Daily Mirror* polled 67,900 in favour of their marrying and 2200 against. It was said that an outdated law that applied only to royal persons should be repealed, and that the remarriage of an innocently divorced man was a practice that merited more congratulation than obloquy. The Queen was not herself blamed, but in long retrospect Ben

Pimlott, her biographer, allowed himself to write, "She might have tried to stop it. There is no evidence that she made such an attempt." She liked Townsend. She did not share her mother's rigorous attitude. She could have argued with the Prime Minister that laws can be changed when the people overwhelmingly desire it, and that consent in so personal a matter should rest with the Queen alone. If the Cabinet insisted on their rights, they should interpret them more liberally, as they did, twelve years later, when Lord Harewood, first cousin to the Queen and a divorcee, was allowed to remarry without fuss. Finally, if Margaret married and was deprived of her Civil List allowance of £15,000 a year, the Queen could well afford to make it good from her own income until Townsend earned an adequate salary. Which was the more important to her – the Church and the Constitution, or her sister's happiness? She chose the former.

Princess Margaret never truly recovered from this blow. Later she married Antony Armstrong-Jones (Lord Snowdon) and they had two children, to whom she was an excellent mother. The marriage ended unhappily, and she never discovered a new role for herself. The Press turned against her, seldom acknowledging her work for charities like the NSPCC, and focusing on her mercurial character, her love affairs, her frequent absences abroad, the icy snubs of which she was capable, her smoking, her drinking, and her apparent lack of any aim. A life needs a strategy as well as tactics, and she seemed to have none. She was never given a proper job, and appeared not to want one. The contrast between her life and the Queen's became more marked as they grew older.

The Duke of Edinburgh's advice on the Townsend affair is unknown. Perhaps he gave none, for the Queen was accustomed to making up her own mind on matters personal to herself. It was the same on politics. While she was supposed to have no political opinions, he had opinions on everything, but was not allowed to express them publicly. He could not be a co-Queen. Constitutionally he did not exist. Nor was he a Consort after the model of Prince Albert who played a prominent political role independent of his wife. Before his marriage he had had a brilliant naval career, but when he was created Admiral of the Fleet, in addition to Field Marshal and Air Chief Marshal, at the Coronation, it must have embarrassed him because he had not earned it. An ambitious man, he was treated by the Court as a difficult Number Two. In his public offices – Founder of the Duke of Edinburgh's Award, of the World Wild Life Fund, of the National Playing Fields Association, and chairman of this society and that – he worked extremely hard at duties which did not win him the acclaim he deserved. He seemed a dynamo that had slipped its driving belt. It was distressing to him that his children, and their children, were to be known as Windsors, not Mountbattens, his family's name. He was a man's man, not a natural subordinate. He excelled at his chosen sports – polo, yachting, piloting aircraft, carriage-driving – but these were elitist sports, which did not earn him popularity.

His discontent became evident in a number of ways. He gained the reputation of a Lothario, unfairly, but he was never photographed in situations and postures which showed his deep affection for the Queen and hers for him. He could be irascible. Meeting him was often a bruising experience, for he did not suffer fools gladly, and as chairman of a committee he was intimidating, largely because his failing was impatience. He was cleverer and sharper than most people, and he did not take kindly to contradiction. Then there was his taste for wardroom humour. The sort of thing he found funny (and so do I) was a welcoming banner strung across a street in India, which read, through typographical error, "A Gal A Day".

He would say what he was thinking, a most unwise thing for famous people to do, for his remarks would be repeated out of context, and teasing which would be accepted from anyone else would be resented coming from him. Some of his reported remarks became famous. To a lady in the rain, "Nobody could look beautiful in this weather, not even you." To an English student in Budapest, "You can't have been here long because you haven't got a pot belly." To a woman solicitor, "I thought it was against the law for women to solicit." In China, to a British student, "If you stay here too long, you will become slitty eyed." To an Australian aboriginal chieftain, "Do you chaps still chuck spears at each other?" And when asked in May 2002 to which part of the Jubilee he most looked forward, he replied, "To August, when it is all over."

These sayings were reported by the Press as the most interesting events of a dull royal day and the Duke naturally came to hate the people who hung around him in the hope of another Philipism. It is unfair that he should be identified with his solecisms but, at the same time, they made him a more lovable figure. *The Times* wrote of him, "He is a specialist in saying the unsayable. He has become a caricature of John Bull. He is a national treasure." Maybe. But if he has commanded popular affection and esteem, it does not go very deep. He could have been the People's Prince, but isn't. He is recognised as a man of substance placed in an anomalous position who has done his duty well. His manner has made him stand out as an individual, and he has contributed an image to the monarchy which is quite different from that of any other royal person, historical or abroad.

The Queen had not been long a queen before her image was challenged by Lord Altrincham in an article he published in 1957 in the *National and English Review* of which he was editor. He did not attack her politics, for she was supposed to have none, but her entourage and her style. He wrote that she surrounded herself with "tweedy" aristocrats, men and women, who had little conception how different post-war England had become. The Court was "a tight little enclave of British ladies and gentlemen" brought up in the same conservative traditions as the Queen herself. To him it seemed absurd that girls of good family were still "presented" at court, like the initiation ceremony of a superior caste. He compared Queen Elizabeth's Court to that of her grandfather, George V, whom he saw as an ideal Monarch, surprisingly "with a classless stamp". Then he turned on the Queen herself. Her style of speaking was, "a pain in the neck. Like her mother she appears unable to string even a few sentences together without a written text... The personality conveyed by the utterances which are put into her mouth is that of a priggish schoolgirl, captain of the hockey team, a prefect, and a recent candidate for Confirmation."

This rhodomontade created an uproar. Altrincham was declared to be a traitor to his class. Here was a young man – Eton and Oxford, a Grenadier, a Conservative candidate for Parliament, who disclaimed his peerage to become John Grigg – daring to criticise the defenceless Queen. He was denounced as a coward and a cad. A man slapped him in the face under the scrutiny of television cameras, and excreta were shoved through his letter box. Archbishop Fisher considered his language "impudent and disrespectful, seeing that he was a private citizen talking about his Sovereign". His behaviour was considered all the more disgraceful because the Queen was about to embark on a tour of Canada and the United States, where his article was widely disseminated.

How far was Altrincham justified? His invective was mainly directed not against the Queen in person but against her Court. It was what they made her say that angered him, not the way she said it. They gave her phrases to utter that could not possibly have come from the mind of a young woman, like a speech at Oxford where she was made to declare, "The University is a powerful fortress against the tide of sloth, ignorance and materialism," which must have made the undergraduates snigger, coming from a woman of their own age. It was true that the Court was drawn from a narrow circle, as was George V's, but they were men and women suited to the task, and it is not surprising that the Queen preferred as her companions people who shared her interests and tastes, and could broaden them, as Patrick Plunket and Peter Townsend did. What was the alternative? To appoint as an equerry a token coloured man from the Commonwealth, or as lady-in-waiting a giddy girl from Cleethorpes, who would be miserable, or as Secretary a man like Altrincham himself who would refuse it? Many changes to Court etiquette were made during her reign – the presentation of debutantes, for instance, was abolished in 1958 – and these were changes proposed by the very people whom Altrincham declared incapable of change. Nevertheless, he enjoyed much support. A motion to expel him from one of his clubs was dismissed with ridicule. My father, a member of the same club, wrote in his diary, "Much of what he said was essentially true," and on Christmas Day that year, after listening to the Queen's broadcast, he wrote, "She spoke with a vigour unknown in pre-Altrincham days."

The most incisive of Altrincham's observations concerned the Queen's public role. He wrote,

When she has lost the bloom of youth, her reputation will depend, far more than it does now, upon her personality. It will not then be enough for her to go through the motions. She will have to say things which people will remember, and do things on her own initiative which will make people sit up and take notice. As yet there is little sign that such a personality is emerging.

This was requiring her to alter not just her methods, but her character. He was urging her to be a queen like the first Elizabeth, to aim for popularity and distinction by displaying in public the mettle of which she was only capable in private – in other words, to be a politician of the calibre of Indira Gandhi or Hillary Clinton, but without the talent or the power.

# V

Of the Queen's dedication and capacity for hard work there can be no two opinions. Every day she receives ten red boxes of State papers, from Downing Street, the Foreign Office, the Ministry of Defence and other Departments, whether she is in Buckingham Palace, Windsor Castle, Sandringham or Balmoral, on duty or on holiday, and she works through them assiduously, annotating as she goes and initialling them "Appr.E.R." as we were permitted to see in one Jubilee film. No example of her disapproval was vouchsafed. Edward Ford has borne witness that she was "wonderful to work for, never complained of another investiture to hold, another Ambassador to greet, a true professional", decisive, courteous, incapable of tantrums. "She never reads a book," said another Secretary, "but when it comes to State papers she is a very quick and absorbed reader – doesn't miss a thing."

Providentially, the most famous Briton in the first half of the last century, and the most famous in the second half, overlapped in office by four years. In 1952 Winston Churchill was seventy-eight, the Queen twenty-six. During the honeymoon period, between her accession and her Coronation, she received him weekly in audience, and they developed the sort of friendship that often occurs between the old and the very young., She enjoyed his reminiscences and jokes, and he her youthful response. It has often been said that he acted like Lord Melbourne to the young Queen Victoria, but it was simpler than that. To her he was fun, and the embodiment of everything that made Great Britain great; to him she was his old-age romance. She commissioned Oscar Nemon to sculpt a portrait bust of him for the Windsor collections, and gave him the Order of the Garter, which he had declined from her father, wishing to remain plain Mr Churchill, not Sir Winston, but he could not refuse it from his daughter.

Not much politics was discussed between them. They preferred talking about their race horses. He seemed to his colleagues obsessed with a single subject, the menace of the H-bomb, and how he alone could alert Soviet Russia to the danger of a world catastrophe. On this topic he made eloquent speeches in the House of Commons, to which I, among a score of newly elected Members, listened with something approaching awe. But when we tried to draw from him his ideas on domestic politics – education, the Health Service, the Beveridge Report – he was uninterested. After one such sticky session in the Smoking Room, he said to an older friend, "Who were those young men talking to me just now? They can't be members of our Party, surely? They're nothing but a set of pink pansies."

On 23 June 1953, only three weeks after the Coronation, he had a massive stroke. His doctor, Lord Moran, told his Private Secretary, Jock Colville, that he was unlikely to survive the weekend. The Queen was informed, and wrote him a guarded letter of sympathy, "I am sorry to hear that you have not been feeling too well." Slowly, against all expectations, he recovered his strength. In September he attended the St Leger with the Queen, and travelled with her to Balmoral, where he spent a few days. He spoke for an hour at the Conservative Party conference at Margate, and began to answer his regular stint of Parliamentary Questions. In December he travelled to Bermuda to discuss the Cold War with President Eisenhower. Only his close colleagues knew of his stroke.

Backbench MPs were quite unaware of it, and the Press barons had agreed to make no mention of it. It seemed to the general public that if he was capable of delivering an oratorical thunderbolt once a month, all was well. But all was not well.

The Queen could have been the one person with the authority to ask him what his intentions were, but she could not bring herself to do so. He wooed her. When she returned from her long Commonwealth tour in May 1954, he met *Britannia* off the Isle of Wight, and sailed with her round the nub of Kent to the Thames estuary and up the river to the heart of her capital, lecturing her all the while on the historic significance of the scenes they were passing. Such gestures entranced her. She was well aware that the reasons he gave for clinging to office (Anthony Eden was not yet well enough to succeed him, and Churchill alone had the prestige to lead a summit conference) were excuses for his reluctance to abandon its delights. He told Moran, "There is no purpose in living once there is nothing to do." Those close to him feared that he was risking both his health and his reputation. Even before his stroke, Colville had noticed that he was visibly ageing ("He finds it hard work to compose a speech, and ideas no longer flow") and Mountbatten that, "he is really past his prime. He is very deaf, and keeps having to have things repeated to him." His consumption of brandy and cigars did his health no good, but he was still capable of reciting from memory fifty lines of Longfellow's "King Robert of Sicily" after a lavish dinner, and warning the House of Commons in his last speech what would happen to the world "if God wearied of mankind", a phrase to which Roy Jenkins drew attention in his biography of Churchill, and which I remember hearing with amazement.

He postponed his resignation again and again, and the Queen made no attempt to hasten it. In March 1955, when he was over eighty, he asked her whether she would mind if he delayed it once more, to which she made no objection. But only a month later he made up his mind to go. At his last audience she said to him kindly, "Would you like a Dukedom or something?" and after some hesitation he declined. On the evening before his resignation he gave a dinner party for her in Downing Street and, in proposing the loyal toast, said that he was using exactly the same formula that he had used as a subaltern sixty years before in drinking the health of her great-great-grandmother. They posed on the steps of Number 10 for a memorable photograph. When Colville went to his bedroom to say goodnight, he found the old man muttering to himself, "I don't believe Anthony can do it."

All her other Prime Ministers and Secretaries have confirmed what Edward Ford said about her dedication. Harold Macmillan was "astonished by her grasp of detail", and Martin Charteris told my father in 1955, "She is one of the most strong-minded and intelligent people I have ever met. Also one of the straightest. If I draft a speech saying 'I am very glad to be here in Hull', she will cross out the 'very' as being an exaggeration." All this is undoubtedly true. What is less credible is that her long experience of politics has given her an insight and wisdom equal or superior to her Ministers'. Her experience is not comparable to theirs. She has to make a multitude of small decisions unaided, but rarely a big one. Politicians have had to struggle throughout their careers to gain their ascendancy; she has not. They are among the ablest people of their generation; which she would not claim to be. Her strength is an emollient one. She calms people. Politicians welcome combat, and expect triumph and disaster. She does not. She is the hub of the wheel, they are on the rim, and hubs move more slowly.

It is therefore not surprising that she cannot talk to

Ministers as their Permanent Secretaries would talk to them, men and women who are also non-party-political, but have had an experience different from hers. It was not to be expected that she could discuss the exchange rate with Harold Wilson or the Budget with Denis Healey with much profit to either of them. Indeed, Healey, who by convention brought her his Budget the day before opening it publicly, said that she had little comment to make on it. It was a formality, and he had to walk backwards after the short interview was over. Then there is her unwillingness to compose her own speeches or speak extempore. Once you judge yourself unable to do it, you develop the habit of relying on other people to do it for you. In private she is a humorous person, but in public she is more appreciative of other people's jokes than making them. Her best witticisms – "I have to be seen to be believed" and, at a dinner given for her at Number 10, "It is nice for the tenants of the tied cottages at either end of the Mall to get together occasionally" – do not bear the stamp of her imagination.

She can be quite fierce, judging by examples Ministers have leaked, such as her reaction to the Spanish government's refusal to allow *Britannia* to dock at Gibraltar during Prince Charles's honeymoon: "It is *my* son, *my* yacht, and *my* dockyard," or when Lord Carrington, the First Lord of the Admiralty, was summoned to the Palace to explain why the yacht was having such an expensive refit: "I see, you will pay, and I will get the blame," as indeed she did. In public she had to guard her tongue carefully. A firm opinion which deviated only marginally from government policy aroused instant protests, like the emphasis she gave to her role in Scotland: "I can never forget that I was crowned Queen of the United Kingdom," when the government was bent on devolution, or a striking phrase in her 1983 Christmas broadcast: "The greatest problem in the world today remains the gap between rich and poor countries, and we shall not begin to close this gap until we hear less about nationalism and more about interdependence," which annoyed Margaret Thatcher, who gave aid to the developing nations a lower priority.

The Prime Minister of the day (she has had ten) has a weekly audience with the Queen, which lasts about an hour. No other person is present, and no record of their conversation is made. The ring of silence that protects the Queen is seldom broken, but reading between the lines of what ex-Prime Ministers have said, we gather that the audiences are neither otiose nor profound. Churchill had not talked politics to her, because she had read the documents and he had not. Macmillan recalled that she would not venture an opinion until she had heard his, and then tentatively. James Callaghan told Elizabeth Longford, "What one gets is friendliness, not friendship. I think she weighs things up, but doesn't offer advice. She listens. She is very interested in the political side – who's going up and who's going down." When he asked her what she would do about a certain problem, she replied, "That's for you to decide. That is what you are paid for." In general, the purpose of these seances is for her to learn more about current affairs than she could gather from the newspapers, and for the Prime Minister to unburden himself and try out his ideas on a receptive mind. John Major found the audiences highly enjoyable: "You can say to her absolutely anything, even things I would not say to the Cabinet."

She had no more difficulty in handling Labour Ministers than Conservative. Indeed, she often found them easier. Heath was correct but "heavy weather", as uninterested in the Commonwealth as she was in his sailing and classical music, and he is on record as being critical of the royal family's extravagant style of living, and wished to cut their Civil List allowance. The most interesting is her relationship with Margaret Thatcher. Although she was the longest serving of her Prime Ministers, we know least about it,

King George V was at first reluctant to broadcast his Christmas messages, but with practice he became a skilled performer, and it was through this medium that he drew closest to his people.

Elizabeth was George V's favourite grandchild, and he was the first to call her Lilibet. Here they are at Balmoral in 1928.

Princess Elizabeth aged ten, 'a distillation of British wholesomeness' (p.19).

The Duke and Duchess of Windsor on their wedding day in 1937. 'Her love for Edward was in doubt, but not her ambition' (p.8).

The royal family in 1942. 'The war, and Churchill, made a king of him' (p. 11).

LEFT George VI's visit to Malta in 1943 was 'the high point of his whole reign' (p. 12).

BELOW The informal style of the royal family in 1943. The Queen rides in a carriage, while the King and Princesses cycle behind.

OPPOSITE PAGE TOP George VI takes the Victory Parade in 1946. Queen Mary sits on the left, determined never to smile in public.

OPPOSITE PAGE BELOW Elizabeth arrives home from Kenya, to be greeted for the first time as Queen by Winston Churchill and other ministers. 'It is one of the most touching photographs taken of her … so young and so very much alone' (p. 18).

ABOVE On her way to open Parliament in 1952, after her accession but before her Coronation. 'How lovely she was as a young woman' (p. 35). OPPOSITE PAGE TOP On the balcony of Buckingham Palace after the Coronation, watching the fly-past. Beside the Queen stand Prince Charles, Princess Anne, the Duke of Edinburgh, the Queen Mother and Princess Margaret. OPPOSITE PAGE BOTTOM On Churchill's resignation in 1955, he gave a farewell dinner party for the Queen at No. 10 Downing Street. 'To her he was fun, and the embodiment of everything that made Great Britain great; to him, she was his old-age romance' (p. 50).

Her Silver Jubilee in 1977. 'We liked to share with the Queen
her evident enjoyment of it' (p. 81).

With her Commonwealth Prime Ministers in 1977, at a banquet
to celebrate her Silver Jubilee. 'Her headship of the Commonwealth is her
most significant political role. Without her, it might not exist.' (p. 77)

because there was extreme reticence on both sides, an indication that it was not entirely a happy one. Mrs Thatcher was "a passionate devotee of the monarchy", as she said of herself, and was always meticulous in her deference to royalty, varying her curtseys from a bob to Fergie to a deep obeisance to the Queen. But she seems to have valued the institution of the monarchy more than she did the person of the Monarch, for whom she felt more respect than admiration. She believed that the Crown should have little to do with the higher functions of the State. She did not wish the Monarch to interfere, or ask too many questions. She thought the weekly audiences an additional duty and, according to one of her staff, her annual trips to Balmoral a nuisance. There was no warmth between the two women. Mrs Thatcher would sit on the edge of her armchair when talking to the Queen, instead of sitting back to enjoy its fullness. They were always correct with each other, but the Queen was constantly made aware that on this chessboard there was only room for one queen, and it was not her. There was no rivalry between them, but their relationship lacked the sympathy that often grew between her and her male Prime Ministers.

Moreover there were differences in attitude between them which were never allowed to surface, but were sufficiently deep for her Private Secretary, Sir William Heseltine, to take the unprecedented step of writing a letter to *The Times* reminding its readers that "the Queen is entitled to have opinions of her own on Government policy, and express them to her chief Ministers", although in the last resort she was bound to accept their decisions. It was not so much substance that divided them, as style. Robert Lacey has written, "A Prime Minister who loved a row was teamed with a Monarch who would do anything to avoid one." For example, while she supported Mrs Thatcher's conflict with the miners, she wished it were less confrontational, and while both were at one in wishing to "de-Socialise" Britain, was the Prime Minister not taking things too fast and behaving a little too arrogantly? She was surprised at being "advised" not to visit Strasbourg, as she had wanted, since Thatcher thought little of the European Parliament and did not want to give it any encouragement. Perhaps, too, the Queen considered herself upstaged by her Prime Minister who hastened to the scene of the Lockerbie air disaster ahead of her, and in taking the salute at the Falklands Victory Parade, when even Winston Churchill took a back seat to the King at the equivalent parade in 1945. In 1982, not a single member of the royal family was invited to the stand.

The difference between the two women is best illustrated by the Commonwealth Conference at Lusaka, Zambia, in August 1979, only a few months after Mrs Thatcher took office for the first time. She was unwilling to attend it, fearing abuse from the African leaders for her quasi-support of Ian Smith's government in Southern Rhodesia. She wanted her Foreign Secretary, Peter Carrington, to take her place, and tried to persuade the Queen not to go. But as the Queen much wanted to go, she had to go too. It was the first time that she had ever visited Africa, whereas the Queen had known many of its leaders like Kaunda of Zambia, Nyerere of Tanzania and Banda of Malawi far longer than they had known each other. She had a benign influence on them. She presided at the opening ceremony, and saw each leader separately to discuss not so much Rhodesia as the problems of his own State, and ask after the welfare of his family. Lee Kuan Yew, Prime Minister of Singapore, put it like this, "Margaret Thatcher was not forthcoming about independence for Rhodesia, but there was this mother figure who represented the wider British public and the Commonwealth, who showed a softer side, a more humane side, and one that sympathised with those aspirations." The Conference began in a mood of antagonism, but she managed to elicit from it an assumption of success. She did not fix anything, but created an atmosphere where fixing was possible. In his memoirs Lord Carrington said that she conferred on the Conference, "a dignity, a sense of occasion and indeed of happiness". In her memoirs Mrs Thatcher mentioned that the Queen was present, but said nothing about her diplomacy. It was, perhaps, the Queen's finest hour. It led directly to the Lancaster House Conference later in the same year, which granted Southern Rhodesia independence as Zimbabwe.

The Labour Ministers were divided in their views on the monarchy according to their upbringing. Those who had risen from the working class (Wilson, Callaghan, Bevan) liked the Queen and attended to her dutifully; those from the middle class (Crossman, Jenkins, Benn, Healey) were less enthusiastic. Crossman's attitude can stand for the others. He supported the monarchy because "it diverted hero-worship into harmless channels", but what was the point of the Queen's Speech at the opening of Parliament when everyone knew it was written for her by the government and announced legislation based on Party doctrines of which she might strongly disapprove? And then this, from his diary, about the ceremony of "kissing hands" on being appointed a Privy Councillor:

I don't suppose anything more dull, pretentious or plain silly has ever been invented. There we were, sixteen grown men, taught for over an hour how to stand up, how to kneel one knee on a cushion, how to raise the right hand with the Bible in it, how to advance three paces towards the Queen, how to take the hand and kiss it, how to move back ten paces without falling over the stools.

He also thought it an absurd anachronism that as Lord

President of the Council he was obliged to travel to Sandringham or Balmoral just to hear the Queen say "Agreed" to fifty Orders in Council. Later he grew quite fond of her personally, and had a grudging respect for her tact. Once he had an audience with her soon after making some disobliging remarks about the monarchy to Lord Porchester, who had repeated them to the Queen. "Ah, Mr Crossman," she said. "Lord Porchester was telling me about you," adding no word of reproach, but making it quite clear that she was aware of his disloyalty. Her mood could change rapidly. After a formal meeting of the Council:

> The Queen was in tremendous form. She described to me a TV programme of a wrestling match at which Philip had been present. An all-in wrestler had been thrown over the ropes, and after writhing in agony, had suddenly shot back into the ring, seized his opponent and forced him to resign. It was interesting to see what a vivid description she gave of the whole scene, writhing herself, twisting and turning, completely relaxed. It was quite an eye-opener to see how she enjoyed it.

That is an attractive picture. She is skilful at making her dignified role acceptable to people who might be contemptuous of it. She is respected for the paradoxical reason that she has good humour but no power.

There does reside in the monarchy, however, a theoretical relic of the prerogatives her forebears used to exercise. First, the power to veto legislation. This has not been used since the reign of Queen Anne, and it is inconceivable that it could be revived today, since it would mean the immediate resignation of the government, followed by a general election in which the Monarch would be involved as a controversial party, which the monarchy would be unlikely to survive. Secondly, the Queen has a vestigial power to summon or dissolve Parliament, but that is now a matter entirely for the government. Thirdly, it is her duty to nominate her Prime Minister in case of doubt, but doubt has been removed by the practice of all political parties to elect their leaders, for whom she is bound to send after an election victory. There was a certain hesitation when Harold Macmillan resigned through ill health in 1963, since there were rival candidates for the succession. But the Queen did not have to make an invidious choice. Soundings were taken among leading Conservatives in the Lords and Commons, and the Queen was advised by Macmillan from his sickbed that Lord Home was favoured above Butler and Hailsham, and she duly invited him to form a government, much to her pleasure, for he was her neighbour in Scotland and she had known him since childhood as a countryman after her own heart. Whether the choice was a wise one was not her concern. Raymond Seitz, a former American ambassador, has well summed up the prerogative question: "The principal Royal Prerogative is the raised eyebrow."

She has other lingering rights. For instance, she could, and did, refuse the publication of her mother's Will and exempt from estate duty her works of art, most of which were exempt in any case. In the main, the Queen's powers are reduced to Walter Bagehot's famous formula, "the right to be consulted, to encourage, and to warn", but not, let it be noted, to advise, let alone to order. The weekly audience with the Prime Minister is stronger evidence of her role in the Constitution than her formal assent to Bills or her "Speech" at the opening of Parliament. The Prime Minister is obliged to justify his policy to her, even though both know that he is unlikely to change it if she disagrees. An example is the Suez crisis of 1956, the most serious of her reign, for the country was deeply divided, not only on Party lines. It is still not certain whether the Queen was aware of the duplicity involved – collusion between Britain, France and Israel, and the suppression of this fact from Parliament, the Commonwealth, the United Nations and the United States – nor has her opinion been subsequently revealed. All we have is Anthony Eden's ambiguous comment, "She understood what we were doing, but I would not claim that she was pro-Suez," which suggests more than doubt in her mind. She may have said to him, "Are you quite sure? What is President Eisenhower's opinion?" but to go further than that, to turn her questions into a statement such as "I think you are making a great mistake" would have provoked a sharp retort and only added to Eden's burden without avail. It would imply that the judgement of a girl still in her twenties was superior to the Cabinet's. Of course she was not without advice, but that too was divided. Adeane was in favour of Suez, Charteris and Ford against. So all she could do was assent by silence and, like the rest of us, look glum.

Another instance, less fundamental, is provided by Ben Pimlott's amusing story of Tony Benn and the postage stamps. He was Postmaster General in Wilson's 1964 government, full of zeal but thwarted by the limited scope of his humble office. A radical and at heart a Republican, he suddenly realised that he had an amazing weapon at his command: he would remove the Queen's head from the postage stamps, a decapitation less terminal than Charles I's, but equally controversial. He was not brash enough to order his office to do this deed without authority higher than his own, but whose authority should he seek? The Queen's, of course. She granted him an audience, and unexpectedly told him that she had no personal feelings about it at all. Emboldened, he showed her a series of designs which omitted her head, arguing that for purely aesthetic reasons her head was superfluous to the design and spoilt it. She made no comment, and thinking that he had received a royal nod of approval, he consulted his officials and the Stamp Advisory Committee, of which Sir Kenneth Clark was Chairman, all of whom were firmly against the idea, not to speak of the courtiers and the Tory Party. He was then made to realise that the Queen may only have appeared to agree because she was constitutionally bound to accept her Minister's advice, even on a matter so personal to herself, and he was given to understand that in fact she hated the idea. The opposition was growing too strong for Tony Benn. Even Harold Wilson would not support him, not on constitutional grounds but because he needed the Queen's help in the crisis that was building up over Southern Rhodesia. Benn was told to shut up. His defeat, however, was not absolute. He managed to shrink the Queen's head to a small black or gold silhouette which he potted into the top corner pocket where, on most stamps, it still remains, to the great disadvantage of the design. Her head in profile, occupying the entire space with no addition except the stamp's value, is what the public wanted and still prefer.

A more serious threat was the continual murmuring about her extravagant style of living, and the burden it imposed on the taxpayer. The secrecy of her finances added to the problem. The public were not permitted to know the value of her possessions, the amount of her personal income or the size of the Treasury's contribution to keep the monarchy in business. It was recognised that no monarchy comes cheap, but was it really necessary for the Queen to inhabit in turn five enormous houses (Buckingham Palace, Windsor Castle, Sandringham, Holyrood House and Balmoral), to maintain a fleet of five Rolls-Royces, two Daimlers and a Bentley to travel between them, and to take with her, for work and on holiday, a staff of eighty? The Queen, in reply, was said to be frugal. She insisted that everyone must turn off the lights when leaving a room. But even if she and Prince Philip dined alone off sausages and mash, it was served by liveried footmen on silver dishes.

The public liked that idea, but they didn't like paying for it. They were confused by the distinction between the Queen's private wealth and income, and money provided for her by the State. If the latter was to pay for her public functions, and the upkeep of her palaces, where was she to draw the line? If she gave a ball to celebrate Prince Charles's twenty-first birthday, was that a private function or a necessary part of royal ceremonial? The people were ambivalent. When they approved, it was called public expenditure; when they disapproved, they called it taxpayers' money. In any case, a large part of her wealth was locked up in her fabulous art collection, which had been slowly accumulated by her ancestors and handed on from Monarch to Monarch. It was inalienable, incapable of being sold, but to the critics inalienable wealth was still wealth, and it seemed to them improper, particularly in periods when the economy was in poor shape, that the Court should ask Parliament for increased subsidies, as if the royal family alone were immune to rising prices. William Hamilton MP, the most outspoken of the critics, described the Crown's latest appeal as "the most brazenly insensitive pay claim made in the last two hundred years".

He did not have the support of the majority of the Labour Cabinet. Their general view was that the Monarch deserved to live in some splendour. "If we have a monarchy," said Aneurin Bevan, "we ought not to lower its standards." To justify the increase demanded, Attlee spoke of the royals as "living the simple life of approachable people", and that they were neither simple nor approachable escaped notice, given the general expectation that the monarchy must be capable of putting on a show. The Select Committee of 1971 endorsed this view. It advocated another rise for the royals, and declared as a matter of principle that the royal style and function should not be lowered.

Slowly the financial facts became known, and adjustments were made. The Queen did not pay tax on her income, nor death duties on her estate. Buckingham Palace and Windsor Castle did not belong to her, but to the State. She owned outright Sandringham and Balmoral, and was responsible for their upkeep. Her private income came mainly from the Duchy of Lancaster, a huge estate of 20,000 acres in the Midlands and the North, which yielded an annual income of £7.3 million. Sandringham was self-supporting, and contributed largely to the upkeep of Balmoral (54,000 acres), which was run at a loss. In addition to the royal art collection, there is the stamp collection (from which a single item, an 1861 Cape of Good Hope, was recently sold for £74,750), and the Queen's jewels, worth £72 million. The Sandringham stud is financed by the Queen herself at a cost of about £450,000 a year. The royal yacht was paid for by the Admiralty, the royal train by British Rail and the Queen's Flight by the Ministry of Defence. The Treasury contributed £7.9 million for exclusively royal duties, salaries and journeys. These are impressive figures, and they did little to modify left-wing opinion when they were revealed. Public reaction was tested in 1992 when the Culture Secretary in John Major's government, Peter Brooke, announced that the cost of repairing Windsor Castle after the disastrous fire would be met from public funds, an assumption which seemed reasonable considering that the Castle was State property and uninsured. His decision was immediately challenged and reversed. The Queen must pay, and she did, by opening Buckingham Palace to the public for the first time. Further changes were set in motion. In 1993 the Queen agreed to pay tax on her private income, and to meet from it the salaries of three of her four children, Charles being financed wholly by the Duchy of Cornwall. Only the Queen, Prince Philip and the Queen Mother, while she lived, were to receive grants from the Civil List. At the same time economies were introduced, like a cut in Buckingham Palace staffs, the shortening of the royal train from fourteen carriages to nine, and greeting cards instead of telegrams are now sent to centenarians. Most important of all, the State subsidy was fixed for ten-year periods instead of being debated annually, thus reducing public curiosity in what royalty was costing year by year. In 2002 its finances were in good shape. Income from its estates was rising, expenditure falling, and in the euphoria of the Jubilee the monarchy's finances became largely immune to political controversy.

In June of that year Sir Michael Peat, Keeper of the Royal Purse, revealed domestic details which went some way – perhaps too far – to palliate lingering criticism. The cost of buying wine for the royal cellar was reduced from £135,000 to £97,000 per annum, and using second-class stamps resulted in an astonishing saving of £400,000. The bottom line for the cost of the monarchy in 2001 was £35.2 million, or 58p per head of population. Stated in those terms monarchy seemed cheap. But it isn't. In that year the royal train, even with its reduced load, cost £675,000 for only fifteen journeys. No commercial firm or government department showed any interest in hiring it.

# VI

WHEN in 1992, her *annus horribilis*, the Queen was asked which she considered the most important of her many functions, she replied, "The investitures." Monarchy should be associated with events done as well as they can be done, and the investitures are done superbly. They take place twenty times a year in Buckingham Palace, once at Holyrood House and once in Cardiff Castle. People of all ranks gather from their distant offices, hospitals, laboratories and universities to receive from the Queen or Prince Charles an honour commensurate with their achievement. It is a great moment for the recipients, and for the three members of their families allowed to accompany them but not to clap.

The ceremony is staged in the ballroom, with beefeaters, Court officials and musicians in attendance, and silence is requested as one by one the honorands stand before the Queen to be knighted by her by touching each shoulder with a naked sword or honoured by looping medals on to little hooks attached to their coat lapels. The Queen, or the Prince of Wales deputising for her, then engages them in a brief conversation. This poses a difficulty, for the royals cannot be expected to know anything about them apart from the one or two who are already public personalities. An equerry steps forward to whisper in the royal ear a name or a word like "Bury St Edmunds" or "formaldehyde" to suggest an opening gambit. One cannot describe the encounter as intimate (when my turn came in later life,

I was growing deaf, and could not hear a word the Prince of Wales uttered) but the formality of it, the splendour of the setting, the quietness of this huge, rich room must for many people represent the culmination of their life's work. For all its solemnity, the ceremony is romantic and joyful. A president's accolade in his private house would not mean the same, let alone a certificate of meritorious service sent to you by post.

Allied to the investitures are the garden parties for those who have already received an honour and those denied one, to give the former a less formal greeting and compensate the latter for their disappointment. Both types feel themselves to be privileged guests instead of miscellaneous people in a queue, and delight in finding themselves in the presence of the Queen in her private garden, with the chance, fairly remote, of speaking to her or at least receiving from her a distant smile. More select are the lunch parties, which she gives several times a year for ten people of assorted professions, perhaps too assorted, because the guest list can include a judge, an Olympic champion, a professor, a businessman, an actress, with little in common except their curiosity to discover why they were invited and who their neighbours at the table are. Groups of people in the same trade who already know each other – writers, academics, engineers, dog lovers – might find these occasions more congenial, but the parties are said to be often jolly.

The more democratic occasions when the Queen meets the people are her periodic tours of different parts of the country. They are not news except locally, where they are stupendous news. They require elaborate organisation, and involve problems of precedence, timing and refreshment. They are also occasions for rejoicing. "The royal family", wrote Bagehot, "sweetens politics by nice and pretty events." While George V was called, sycophantically,

"Father of the People", it would be absurd to nominate the Queen as their mother. That is not her style. She endows these events with benevolence, but keeps her reserve. Her walkabouts are brief. She passes the endless bouquets to ladies-in-waiting. She is not naturally a crowd pleaser. She has the problem of what expression to put on while the national anthem is being played – grateful, hopeful, solemn or happy. The stress of being the centre of attention by many thousands for many hours on end is great. Sir Michael Adeane thus expressed it when giving evidence to the Select Committee on the Civil List in 1970:

> The strain of a long day in a provincial town, taking a lively interest in everything, saying a kind word here and asking a question there, always smiling and acknowledging cheers when driving in her car, sometimes for hours, has to be experienced to be perfectly appreciated.

To everyone in the crowd it is a unique event; to her it is a repetition of the event before. People are not at their best on such occasions. They simper. Out of nervousness, and in an effort to act "naturally" they can be impertinent. She knows that everything she says will be endlessly repeated, so she says nothing of any interest. She has no chance of getting to know any of the hundreds who press around her, and the Mayor's exegesis of the history and virtues of his town is lost in the general cacophony. If the Duke of Edinburgh accompanies her, he is of much help, but he cannot conceal his boredom with superficial events. He speaks angrily to reporters, and risks making sharp remarks, often with unhappy consequences. The Queen is calmer. Unlike the Duke and film stars, she has never known what it is like to be unknown.

Fame has never been her spur; always her burden. She has encountered every situation many times before – the awkward lord lieutenant, the verbose chairman of a factory or museum, the shy children, amateur choruses and dances, endless banquets – and can cut them short without discourtesy. She never shows off. She remains her own person. She is always pleasant, but never comic. She does not make jokes. She does not kiss babies. Long ago she crossed the borderline that divides respect from affection, but has yet to penetrate the higher barrier between affection and love. Love involves propinquity, such as came easily to Diana, Princess of Wales. The Queen does not touch, nor consent to be touched. It is important to her that we do not get to know her too well, and she does not ingratiate herself to us. Gifted with remarkably good health and stamina, and with an actress's determination that the show must go on, she never chucks an engagement and is never late for one. She may not be indefatigable, but seems so, and if she does not enjoy doing what she has to do, she puts on a good pretence of enjoying it.

Her reticence had gained her the reputation of being stiff and remote, and to correct this impression she consented in 1968, at first a little reluctantly, to the BBC's request to make a documentary film of her family life, which would give them a cosier image. There was some hesitation on both sides. David Attenborough, who was then in charge of documentaries, warned Richard Cawston, the producer-director, "You're killing the monarchy with this film. The whole institution depends on mystique and the tribal chief in his hut. If any member of the tribe sees into the hut, then the whole system of the tribal chiefdom is damaged." He was overridden by Mounbatten and Prince Philip who persuaded the Queen to accept the idea. It would humanise the family, they said. It would show that their fabulous life was not necessarily dull. It would de-iconise the Queen without making her too accessible. It would have the quality of a home movie. The danger was that they might appear too human to be worthy of so exalted a rank, and that the film would set a precedent for even deeper intrusion into their private lives. If the BBC could film them at home, why not the paparazzi too?

The Duke of Edinburgh took control. He had the right of suggestion and the right of veto. Filming took place over a whole year, 1968–9, but not continuously. Only forty-three hours were shot, of which only ninety-three minutes were actually broadcast. At first there were inevitable strains. The Queen was startled to find a furry microphone thrust under her nose as she was talking to a Commonwealth Prime Minister, and the Duke was once so enraged that he shouted, "Keep that bloody camera away from the Queen!"

He also vetoed filming the family when they were engaged in field sports, lest the public complain that they spent their time killing birds and hunting animals. The emphasis was to be on the family's public duties and home life. The Queen was seen at work with her Secretary, on State visits abroad, shopping and barbecuing at Balmoral, spending Christmas at Windsor. Some of the film would be too ordinary to be interesting were it not that the main actors were extraordinary people, and some of it was a little cruel, like the gormlessness of Prince Charles, aged nineteen, and the pomposity of the American ambassador, Walter Annenberg, who on being asked by the Queen whether he was happy with his accommodation in London, replied, "We are in the Embassy residence, subject of course to some of the discomfiture as a result of a need for elements of refurbishing and rehabilitation," but all senior Americans speak like that on formal occasions. The Queen had no such difficulty. In private she speaks as members of the upper class have always spoken: "What? Three sausages! Don't be greedy." "But one owes oneself a treat from time to time."

A few months after the first showing of the film came the investiture of Charles as Prince of Wales. He had held that title since 1958, when his mother announced it as a birthday surprise, and he first heard of it on the radio at his preparatory school. It did not give him as much joy as she had hoped, since his schoolfellows ridiculed him, adding their own ribald versions to his other titles, Duke of Cornwall and Rothesay, Earl of Carrick, Baron of Renfrew, Lord of the Isles, Great Steward of Scotland and Earl of Chester. He was only nine years old. In 1969 the ceremony was a reaffirmation of his title, and a "presentation" of their Prince to the people of Wales. It was one of those events by which the monarchy periodically renews itself by recalling its ancient origins and staging for the people a memorable show which in any but a royal context would seem overdramatic and absurd.

The investiture had another purpose too. It was to reaffirm the indivisibility of the United Kingdom. Between 1958 and 1969 Welsh nationalism had gained much support, and Plaid Cymru were winning seats which the Labour Party could ill afford to lose. Let there be a demonstration of national unity under the guise of a royal investiture to which few people would object. Another significance of the event was not lost on the Welsh. It was staged at Caernarvon Castle, one of a chain of fortresses built by Edward I to subdue the Welsh and symbolise the conquest of Wales. The Queen's message was in effect, "We, the English, recognise your culture and your history, and we give you our son to be your Prince." This was acceptable to the great majority, and there were fewer hostile demonstrations than expected. Two patriot-terrorists killed themselves while placing their explosives under a bridge thirty miles from Caernarvon, and there were spasmodic boos along the processional route. Security was as tight as was consistent with the pageantry. It had been seriously apprehended that an attempt might be made on the Prince's life, and he accepted the risk with equanimity.

The investiture was stage-managed by Lord Snowdon, the Queen's brother-in-law, with an unprecedented mixture of medieval romanticism and twentieth-century high tech. The thirteenth-century castle, with its crenellations, towers and massive walls, might have been built as a film set, but was almost the only genuine feature of the whole performance. In the central courtyard Snowdon built a low stage on which were placed three thrones of Welsh slate surmounted by a canopy of transparent Perspex to allow the television cameras a clear view. The Queen wore clothes of her own date and style, but the Prince was dressed as a medieval page, escorted by six Welsh peers bearing his insignia. A degree of play-acting was required of both Queen and Prince, switching from "Oh my goodness, I must have left my brolly in the loo", to "Sir Constable, I return the key of the Castle into your keeping" (the Constable being Snowdon himself), and this cannot be managed without giggling unless the actors are profoundly convinced of its significance.

Prince Charles certainly was. The moment when he swore his oath of fealty to his mother was deeply moving. In 1911, his great-uncle David, later Edward VIII, had thought the ceremony ridiculous and his knee-breeches "a preposterous rig" but Charles entered into the spirit of the event, and because he was so evidently moved by it, and enjoyed it, he swayed people's emotions in his favour. When he and the Queen appeared on the balcony overlooking the town's main square, it was an intensely stirring sight to the crowds and to the millions watching on television around the world. The justification of the whole venture came in the following days when Charles travelled to every part of his principality and was acclaimed everywhere. It was an undoubted success. People who had expected to like it, liked it. Those who didn't, didn't. Most did.

# VII

THE Prince's investiture was designed to make the British monarchy acceptable to one of the kingdom's constituent parts. But the Queen's role as ambassador extends around the world. As hostess she is obliged, several times a year, to receive other monarchs and heads of state on State visits to London. The crowds that line the Mall under the flags of the visiting potentate are thick or thin, depending on the importance and current popularity of his country. When President Heuss of the Federal Republic of Germany came in 1958, his reception was cool, and when the Queen turned to him and indicated a group who raised a tolerable cheer in his honour, he replied with a tact and humour that endeared him to her, "eighty-five per cent of the cheers are for Your Majesty; the others are for the horses." His visit was of some political importance, since it was the first by a German head of state after the war. Although his gift of £5000 towards the rebuilding of Coventry Cathedral was thought inadequate, and the Queen's reference at the banquet to her family's ancestral links with Germany did not go down well with the public, the Emperor Hirohito of Japan, who came three years later, suffered more. As he and the Queen drove down the Mall in an open carriage, Sarah Bradford reminds us, there were hostile shouts from the crowd. "I'm glad the Emperor couldn't understand English," the Queen confided later. Even less welcome was President Nicolae Ceauşescu of Romania, who anticipated his unpopularity in Britain by sending ahead his own security men to check the panelling and light fittings of the suite allotted to him in Buckingham Palace.

Other visitors, like President Walesa of Poland, were awkward because they could not speak a word of English, and the splendour of the setting at Windsor contrasted with the poverty of the conversation. American presidents, especially Reagan, were not similarly handicapped and were doubly welcome. But the Queen was adept at entertaining the most difficult of guests. William Rees-Mogg, a former editor of *The Times*, was once invited by her to lunch with the President of the Ivory Coast:

The Queen showed one quality of a gifted actress [he wrote]. She knows how to control the tempo of a scene. One could say that she played the lunch party as though it were a light comedy – perhaps in the style of Noël Coward. She made it welcoming, friendly, humorous and yet sufficiently various to please the President, who had a great deal of charm himself. ... Her sense of occasion has been a skill by which the Commonwealth has been held together.

So much for the Queen as hostess. The Queen as guest alternates between visits to Commonwealth countries where she is still Monarch or head of state, and countries where she is a foreigner. For both functions the royal yacht *Britannia* was paramount, and the meanness of Parliament in not replacing her when she was decommissioned in 1997 was very short-sighted. She was built on Clydebank in 1953 not as a yacht, but as a luxury ship, with a crew of 250 under an admiral, and staterooms for occupation and entertainment. She was not large – 5769 tonnes – but she looked larger. In her forty-four years of service, she visited over 600 ports in 135 countries. For overseas voyages she had many advantages. The head of a great maritime nation must arrive in style. *Britannia* provided the royal family with familiar rooms to which they could return again and again without packing and unpacking. She was a floating five-star hotel, in which they could rest between formal engagements ashore. She contained splendid reception rooms in which to return hospitality. She impressed the grandest of foreign grandees, their diplomats and businessmen. *Britannia* fulfilled all these roles. She was an advertisement for our country, and a demonstration of why our monarchy is valued.

The Queen has visited almost as many countries as there are countries to visit. She was the first British Monarch to go to Soviet Russia and Communist China. Everywhere she was received with curiosity and delight, as much for her own person as for her rarity, as the Mikado might have been welcomed to London in 1850. Douglas Hurd, who accompanied her as Foreign Secretary, has said, "She evoked a sort of nostalgia, a sort of envy ... It was remarkable in Russia, where they were groping for their own past." Her visits always had some political significance, although she never talked politics, like her return visit of conciliation to Germany in 1965, when in ten days she toured the whole country by train, and the East Berliners peered at her over the Wall, or, less happily, to Morocco in 1980, where King Hussan kept her waiting for lunch till 3.40 p.m., while the whole world watched her growing impatience on television. She was treated everywhere as the most important State visitor of the year, and the deference of her hosts must often have been cloying. As a young woman she never met her contemporaries abroad. Her escorts were presidents, ministers and ambassadors. She could never wander anonymously with a friend through the streets of Rome or Katmandu. She must carefully avoid controversy ("That is very interesting, Mr President. I am sure our Foreign Secretary would like to pursue the matter with you") and appear always at her best, in dress, manner and deportment, when she longed to act as a tourist might act.

It was different in the United States. Formality was not lacking there – she was the first British Monarch to address a joint meeting of both Houses of Congress, soon after the Gulf War – but it was the warmth of the American welcome that entranced her. Americans are fascinated by royalty, particularly by British royalty for its relevance to their own history, and for its strangeness and glamour. In contrast to Europeans and Asians, they are quite uninhibited. Jonathan Dimbleby quotes an example from Prince Charles's journal of his visit to California in 1974:

"OK. You're a Prince, right?"
"Yes, quite right," I replied.
"Say, does that mean you become a king one day, is that the deal?"
"Well, I ... eh ... suppose so," I stuttered.

Americans love celebrities, and there is no greater celebrity than a queen, who may be isolated by her elevated position, but is nonetheless treated as a person. She responded to their enthusiasm by her own, as we all do when buoyant with success. To coincide with her visit to New York in 1957 Malcolm Muggeridge, with unforgivable caddishness, published in the *Saturday Evening Post* an article that attacked the monarchy as obsolete and the Queen as "dowdy, frumpish and banal". It did her nothing but good, for her youthful manner and appearance proved the opposite. On a later visit to California she insisted on riding to President Reagan's ranch in a heavy downpour. She is adept at responding to people's moods. Some of her tributes to America, whether her own or suggested to her, are truly memorable, like her words of sympathy to the bereaved after 11 September 2001, "Grief is the price we pay for love," and ordering the Guards band to play the "Star Spangled Banner" in the forecourt of Buckingham Palace on the same occasion.

Her headship of the Commonwealth is her most significant political role. Without her it might not exist. She is given insufficient credit for the trouble she has taken to hold it together. Sadly, what means most to her means least to her subjects. Her Prime Ministers have not given it the attention, and rarely the affection, that came naturally to her. I remember Harold Macmillan, at a private dinner of backbench MPs, saying to us,

> Tomorrow I have got to meet the Commonwealth Prime Ministers. They will expect me to say that we will invest £100 million in their countries. Four black faces, six white faces, will look at me expectantly. What am I to tell them? Has it any meaning at all, this assembly of such different nations?

To the Queen it did have a meaning. It gave Britain a wider role in world affairs enjoyed by no other monarchy. It was an inoffensive reminder of our Imperial past. She had sworn at her Coronation, "to govern, according to their respective laws and customs, the peoples of the United Kingdom and Northern Ireland, Canada, Australia, New Zealand, the Union of South Africa, Pakistan and Ceylon, and all our possessions and other territories to any of them belonging or appertaining". There was no mention of Empire or Commonwealth, but it was implied. The term "to govern", though meaningless, was accepted as a symbol binding a free association of independent members, numbering fifty-four today, nearly a third of the membership of the United Nations. It is a political phenomenon without parallel.

Its membership is remarkably stable. Most countries that were part of the Empire remain in the Commonwealth. Some, like Ireland and Burma, never joined. Others, like Papua New Guinea, which were never in the Empire, joined the Commonwealth voluntarily. Some, like Pakistan, withdrew, only to apply for readmission. South Africa withdrew in 1961 when it became clear to her government that apartheid was incompatible with Commonwealth membership, and in 1994 rejoined when President de Klerk and Nelson Mandela remedied this injustice. Others, like Fiji, Zimbabwe and Nigeria, were temporarily suspended. The Commonwealth was undoubtedly a moral force in the world, as Britain found to her own cost when the great majority of Commonwealth countries voted against us at the time of the Suez crisis in 1956. What, then, constitutes the bond? It is an historical legacy of a past of which we have no reason to feel ashamed. It transcends barriers of race. It gives the smaller countries – some of them mere islands scooped up by eighteenth-century adventurers – an importance and security which they would otherwise have lacked, like the Falklands in 1982. Its members share memories of both World Wars, when they were close allies of Great Britain, and after Dunkirk her only ones. The paradox that the Queen was "head" of several self-governing Republics was for a time unquestioned.

In the year after her Coronation, the Queen and Prince Philip undertook the longest Commonwealth tour of her reign. It lasted nearly six months and took them in HMS *Gothic*, before *Britannia* was commissioned, 43,000 miles, to Jamaica, Fiji, Tonga, New Zealand, Australia (for two months), Ceylon, Malta and Gibraltar. Everywhere they were greeted with astonishment. Everyone had seen them on television. Here they were in person – the Queen in her youthful beauty, Prince Philip the model of what a young man should be. Inevitably such euphoria was unlikely to be repeated. Visits became shorter, usually by air, and the novelty wore off. The crowds diminished, tour by tour, especially in the "old" Empire, where pride of independent nationhood began to take precedence over loyalty to a distant Crown. Australia and New Zealand found it difficult to maintain the fiction that she was Queen of a State of which she was not even a national, and where she had no permanent home.

Britain was turning more to Europe and the United States, now that the Antipodes were of less strategic and economic importance to her. Slowly links were severed. The right of appeal to the Privy Council was abolished. "God Save the Queen" was replaced by "Advance Australia Fair". The proportion of British-born in Australia's population decreased under the influx of Asian and other nationalities. In New Zealand, in 2002, 58 per cent of the people were pro-monarchy, 38 per cent for a Republic. In Canada the situation was complicated by the French separatist movement. Hostility to a British monarchy was so prevalent in Quebec that the security on royal tours was increased to the extent of making the Queen almost inaccessible, which diminished the enthusiasm of the loyal majority. Her role, in any case, was little more than titular. Since 1952 the Governor General has been a Canadian, owing only mythological duty to her. Canadian trade with Britain has lessened in favour of the United States as rapidly as British trade gravitated to Europe. Allegiance to the Crown remains an emotional link, but it is weakening.

The most surprising situation is in Africa. Sixteen black African nations accept the Queen as head of state, although they were the countries most proud of gaining their independence and were often resentful of past colonial rule. Although many have suffered from political inexperience and some tyrannical rulers, the Queen has found herself at ease with them. Her very presence, as at Lusaka, acts as a calming influence. Charles Douglas-Home has put it well: "She does good by stealth." It is impossible to continue acrimonious debate while they are her guests. She takes great pains to memorise her briefings. Sir Sonny Ramphal, one-time Commonwealth Secretary-General, has said,

> She would know who was in the clutches of the IMF [International Monetary Fund], who had got what political scandal raging, she'd know the family side of things, if there were children or deaths in the family. She'd know about the economy, she'd know about Elections coming up. They felt they were talking to a friend who cared about the country.

An excellent example of her influence was her visit to Ghana in 1961. Doubts on whether she should go there were expressed in Parliament on two grounds. First, her life would be at risk, not because an attempt might be made on her personally, but on President Nkrumah, in whose close company she was bound to spend much of her time. Second, her visit might seem to endorse one of the most corrupt regimes in Africa. On the other hand, cancellation of the visit might seem weak, and drive Nkrumah further into the arms of Soviet Russia, adrift from the Commonwealth. Two people must make the decision whether she should go or not, Harold Macmillan, the Prime Minister, and the Queen herself. Macmillan with some apprehension, urged her to go. He told President Kennedy, "I am risking my Queen," as if it were a game of chess. The Queen insisted on going, saying she did not know how she would carry on if she were prevented from going. Macmillan recorded in his diary, "She has been absolutely determined all through... She is impatient of the attitude towards her to treat her as a *woman*, or a film star or mascot. She knows her duty, and means to be a Queen, not a puppet."

So she went. The visit was a tremendous success. The Ghanaians, Republicans to a man, cheered her enthusiastically. A local newspaper hailed her as "the world's greatest Socialist monarch". She was photographed dancing with Nkrumah. The only damage done to either of them was an explosion that ripped off the legs of the President's statue in Accra, but this was before the Queen arrived. The whole incident illustrates her fortitude, and the unique place she holds in the Commonwealth. She is reported to have said, "How silly I should look if I was scared to visit Ghana, and then Khrushchev went and had a great reception." She was well aware that although she might be a Queen, on the diplomatic chessboard she was also a pawn.

Her African tours were not much reported in Britain, unless something went amusingly wrong with the arrangements or the Queen was thought to have been insulted. But although little noticed, her dedication and avoidance of diplomatic error boosted her standing at home, and this was recognised in her Silver Jubilee of 1977. Royal Jubilees implicitly ask two questions of the people: "Have I done the job OK?" and "Is the job worth doing?" To the first question the answer was unanimous in her favour. The second was sidestepped. In the general euphoria, it was almost improper to ask it. But the country was in the middle of an economic slump: 1½ million were unemployed. Were we in the mood to celebrate anything? The Court feared a flop. In the event, it was a great success. The golden coach was wheeled out once more and trundled to St Paul's between cheering crowds. The nation surprised itself by its enthusiasm. This was partly because we liked to share with the Queen her evident enjoyment of it. When she lit the initial beacon on Snow Hill at Windsor, the first of a chain of beacons that encircled the kingdom, she had never looked happier. It was also a good excuse for a party. But you do not stand for hours in the rain to have a fleeting glimpse of a woman in a car unless she stands for something more and is a woman worthy of affection. That was her reward.

# VIII

MORE is known about Prince Charles's youth than almost any other man's, for he has been the object of curiosity and Press attention since his earliest boyhood, and of reminiscence ever since. His letters, however childish, have been quoted at length, his friends interviewed, and his biography, of which he was himself a collaborator, has been written in explicit detail by Jonathan Dimbleby, to whom I am indebted for much of the information that follows.

He has said of himself, "I am an ordinary person in an extraordinary position," but his position prevented him from being ordinary. He could never escape his future. Since his parents were unlike any other parents, he never established with them the easy familiarity that comes with the rough and tumble of a normal home life. In his childhood he was guided not so much by them as by nannies and governesses. His mother was too busy, and too often abroad, and being herself a reticent person, gave the impression of aloofness, leaving his upbringing largely to his father. Here, too, there was a difficulty. Charles was a shy boy, and Prince Philip imagined that he could cure his shyness by being rough with him and putting him at psychological jumps that the boy was unable to clear. He was not starved of affection, but there was a certain emotional reserve. A shy boy should be encouraged by being told that shyness is a temporary handicap, not a permanent disability, and that a person who is not shy in youth will become intolerable in middle age. Dimbleby puts Charles's early family relationships astutely: "Impatience on one side, and trepidation on the other." Charles's diffidence did have one advantage, that as he was shy of people as a boy, he knew what it meant when people were shy of him as an adult.

It is hard to imagine the proper education for a boy of his rank and future role. He could not be taught by governesses at home, like his mother and aunt. He must go to a boarding school. Prince Philip chose what had been his own preparatory school, Cheam in Berkshire, a school of eighty-five boys between the ages of eight and fourteen, where Charles spent five, largely unhappy, years. He was not a failure – he ended up as head boy – but he did not, and could not, mix with the other boys in easy comradeship, because of his nature, and because he arrived at Cheam as Duke of Cornwall and in mid-term was created Prince of Wales by his mother. He did not stand much of a chance. His insecurity was not overcome by moderate success at games and academic work. It is tempting to think of him as studious, but he showed little sign of the intellectual curiosity that in later life distinguished him from the rest of his family. His lonesome and somewhat eccentric character is well illustrated by an anecdote that can only have been told to Dimbleby by Prince Charles himself:

In the spring of 1957 [when he was eight] his tonsils were removed and preserved in a glass jar. For several weeks the Prince insisted on taking them with him wherever he went. At Windsor he had conceived an affection for the little chapel that lay between the Grand Corridor and St George's Hall. There, alone, he would stand in the pulpit delivering sermons to an imaginary but rapt congregation. On one occasion he was so taken by his own performance that he swept out into the Grand Corridor – forgetting that he had left his tonsils on the pulpit.

He most enjoyed Balmoral, its lakes, mountains, wildlife and solitude, and to his father's relief, took to shooting and riding, but never with the high spirits of Princess Anne. It is not pleasant for a boy to hear his father say that he wished his son were more like his sister.

The next stage in Charles's education was a disaster. Prince Philip could have sent him to Eton, where he would have been under the guidance of sensitive masters, have a room of his own, and be subject to a regime better suited to his temperament. But he once again chose his old school, Gordonstoun, in Scotland, where the regime was Spartan to a fault and inconsiderate to the point of brutality. An old boy, Ross Benson, later wrote that it was the custom to truss up new boys in a wicker laundry basket and leave it for hours under a dripping cold tap. Another contemporary, William Boyd, the novelist, speaks of gangs of boys roaming the house after dark, beating up smaller boys, extorting food and money from them, and creating an atmosphere of genuine terror. The coarseness of their behaviour and language appalled young Charles, who was treated as an object for ridicule and torment, particularly on the rugger field, where brutal tackling could be disguised as sport. It added spice to their enjoyment that their victim was their future king. To complain to the masters would only invite further retribution. He made no friends, because there was nobody who was prepared to risk contempt for sucking up to the Prince. His friendlessness was made more painful by his total lack of privacy. Everywhere he was followed by a personal detective, and he slept in a dormitory with fourteen other boys. In his pathetic letters home he begged to be taken away. Philip replied that he must stick it, with the implication that it would make him a man of the right stuff. So for three grim years he stuck it, finding consolation in art, music (particularly the cello) and, surprisingly, acting. He had the comfort of one individual, the arts master, who understood and sympathised with him.

His next educational stepping stone was a temporary secondment to Australia, to give him a taste of the Commonwealth and accustom him to hardship of a more acceptable kind than school bullying. At the age of seventeen he spent several months at Timbertop school, in the outback a hundred miles north-east of Melbourne. As usual, the Press were implored to treat the Prince as a normal schoolboy, but his celebrity as their future king ensured that on arriving by air at Sydney he was greeted by the Prime Minister, the Governor General and 320 assorted Press. Thereafter things improved. Timbertop was not unlike Gordonstoun, indeed modelled on it, but the mood was more congenial to him, and because more time was spent in the open air than in the classroom, he grew in confidence, taking part in arduous expeditions into the surrounding wilderness.

He spent weekends with the family of David Checketts, Prince Philip's Secretary, who went to Australia with him as companion-adviser, and formed a lasting friendship with him. One of his more adventurous expeditions was to Papua New Guinea, where he was unmolested by the gentle people, and found among them a tenderness that matched his own. One of them recorded this remarkable tribute to him: "He came among us as if in a cage, and before our eyes he has become free." Checketts went further: "I went out with a boy, and came back with a man."

It was a kindly tribute, but premature. Charles still had to endure a final year at Gordonstoun, and his former reticence took control again. He was appointed head boy, a title that gave rise to cynical laughter, for he was ill equipped for it. A letter which he wrote home in April 1967 reveals his continuing insecurity:

There is a dance here in a fortnight's time which fills me with horror as I have to arrange most of it. The idea is so awful as thirty girls are being transported from an Aberdeen school to provide material for dancing. I shall do my best not to dance or become involved.

Perhaps this was written in order to protect himself from family curiosity about his interest in girls, for, as it turned out, he danced with several of them.

Then came Cambridge. Charles was barely consulted. His future was planned by his father and Mountbatten, who thought that after his unhappy experiences at school, he deserved the relaxation and comradeship of a university. How different he was from his sister Anne! She had been happy at Benenden school, at ease with her companions, although they were addressed as Isabel and Jane, and she as Princess, and she left with two moderate A-levels to her credit, a passion for sports, and no desire whatever to go to a university. She would devote her youth to equestrian events, eventually reaching Olympian level. Charles, meanwhile, went to Trinity College, pursued by the Press until they had had their fill of photo opportunities, and there he studied archaeology and anthropology (in his second year, history), and began to make friends in a saner environment. He still did not find it easy. There was the obstacle of his title, the continual presence of a detective, and his own self-deprecating reserve. He joined societies, acted in university plays, invited fellow undergraduates to shoot at Sandringham, and met Lucia Santa Cruz, the daughter of the Chilean ambassador and research assistant to Rab Butler, Master of the College, who allowed himself to say, with typical indiscretion, that he had, "facilitated a liaison, in the course of which the young South American had instructed an innocent Prince in the consummation of physical love".

In the middle of his Cambridge course he spent a term at Aberystwyth to gain some credibility for his coming investiture at Caernarvon. What chance did a "Prince of Wales" have among a rowdy group of Welsh students who resented both his title and his presence? "I haven't made a lot of friends," he said in his first television interview. "In this sense, I suppose, I have had a lonely time." He found it impossible to dissimulate. He was considered, and considered himself at this stage of his life, unfit for high office, let alone the highest.

His next destination was the Navy. His father and great-uncle hoped that it would stiffen his resolve, as it had their own. It is difficult to realise that Prince Charles spent five years of his early life at sea, so firmly is he now associated with the land. It was a formative period of his life, just as the Second World War was for many civilians who joined the armed services for the duration and now regard their experience as irrelevant to their later careers, though it left a mark on their characters. If Prince Charles had been guided away from the Navy into the byroads of industry, business or politics, it is doubtful that he would have gained so much knowledge of human nature and foreign countries as he did in the Royal Navy. We know a great deal about his naval career and how it affected him, because he was obliged to keep a journal, which was scrutinised by his commanding officers, and he wrote many letters to his chief mentor and father substitute, Lord Mountbatten.

Their relationship grew in intensity as Charles came to rely on him for private tuition in the intricacies of naval sciences, and at a more human level for advice on conduct, moral principles, and relations with superiors and subordinates. They formed so close an intimacy that Charles touched in his great-uncle a more tender chord, and he in Charles a capacity to make his own decisions and to relax. "What a really charming young man he is," Mountbatten wrote in his diary, and to Charles he wrote, "I've been thinking of you – far more than I had ever expected to think of a young man, but then I've got to know you so well, I really miss you very much."

Slowly, and with infinite tact, Mountbatten invited young women to Broadlands, when Charles was there on leave, to enliven their bachelor society, and Charles fell in love with one of them, Camilla Shand. Dimbleby thus describes her appeal:

> She was pretty, bubbly, and she smiled with her eyes as well as her mouth. Unlike some others he had met, she lacked coquetry, and did not preen herself. She laughed easily, and at the same sillinesses that brought him to tears of laughter. ... His taste for the absurd was complemented by her down-to-earth irreverence. Not caring for fashion or style, she was at home in the country with horses and hunting. ... She was affectionate, she was unassuming, and – with all the intensity of first love – he lost his heart to her almost at once.

Mountbatten did not encourage this romance. He saw Camilla more as a temporary girlfriend than as a future wife. In his eyes, she was not sufficiently virginal or aristocratic to become Queen, and in any case he had his own candidate, his granddaughter Amanda Knatchbull. Charles's naval duties took him away from Camilla. He had hesitated to propose to her because he was so young and, in the long interval, he lost her. He was overseas for eight months, and it was when his ship was at anchor in the Caribbean that he heard she was engaged to marry Andrew Parker Bowles. He recorded in his diary his "feeling of emptiness". He was only twenty-three.

Before going to Dartmouth for his naval training, he spent five months at the RAF training college Cranwell, and learnt to fly proficiently enough to win his wings. He found himself sharing with other young men the arduous and nerve-testing ordeals of first solo flights and parachute jumping that formed a close bond between them. But at Dartmouth he was back at school again, subject to regulations that seemed to him unnecessary and absurd. He was not a born midshipman. He found navigation a skill particularly difficult to master, and it was only because he had in his great-uncle so expert and patient a tutor that he managed to pass his exams with sufficient credit to justify his posting to a man-of-war, HMS *Norfolk*, then lying at Gibraltar.

It is not necessary to follow his naval career in detail. Suffice to say that it took him to all the home ports, to every part of the Mediterranean and Baltic, to the West Indies, the Atlantic coast of South America and both ocean coasts of the United States. He also had some experience of the Fleet Air Arm and of submarines. At first he felt inadequate. "I am afraid I tend to suffer from bouts of hopeless depression, because I feel I'm not going to cope," he wrote to Mountbatten. Surrounded by professional officers who had careers to make when his had been settled for him since birth, and being simultaneously a sub-lieutenant and a Royal Highness, he found at first greater companionship with the seamen who shared his love of ribaldry and were not shy of speaking of their home lives. His natural gentleness and dedication to the job won him affection and respect. He never learnt more than the rudiments of navigation, much as a middle-aged man finds it hard to master a computer beyond its elementary stages, but he became proficient enough during those five years to be entrusted with the command of the humblest vessel in his mother's fleet, HMS *Bronington*, a coastal minesweeper with a crew of thirty-three. Knowing what the Press would make of any accident to his ship, and the awful prospect of the heir to the throne being court-martialled for running her on the rocks, he was naturally scared on taking over his first and only command.

Though *Bronington*'s role was modest, and in peacetime almost redundant, he was obliged to guide her through the most dangerous inland waters searching for non-existent mines. No disaster occurred, and when he left the Navy his final report acknowledged without sycophancy, "He has attained an excellent level of professional competence, and has shown a deep understanding for his sailors and their families, and as a result the morale of his ship has been of an extremely high order." One illustration of his style of leadership can end this brief summary. A seaman was brought before him for repeatedly outstaying his leave. The man explained that after his last offence he had bought two alarm clocks to wake him up in time. Unfortunately his wife's budgerigar settled on each clock in turn and switched off the mechanism. Charles listened to this preposterous excuse with a straight face and dismissed the man without comment, to the consternation of the ship's coxswain who had suggested a severe punishment. But the crew loved him for it, and on the day of his departure in 1976 carried him ashore at Rosyth in a wheeled chair and trundled him past all the other naval ships whose crews joined in the cheering. He had left, but in another sense he had arrived.

What was Prince Charles to do with his life until he succeeded his mother? Most of it was ordained. He would undertake duties suitable for a Prince of Wales, attending functions at home and abroad, and standing in for the Queen when she desired it. No other profession was open to him. He could not govern one of the old Dominions, for they insisted on a Governor of their own nationality. He could head innumerable charities, but was not in day-to-day control even of the Prince's Trust or the United World

College to which he attached most importance, nor of the Duchy of Cornwall which provided his entire income. In public he never wavered from his duties, believing that if you have to do something, however repetitive or wearisome, there is no point in doing it with obvious reluctance. His tantrums he reserved for his staff, and was liable to unpredictable and often inexplicable rages. He was scarcely on speaking terms with the Buckingham Palace courtiers. When Lord Mountbatten was killed by an Irish terrorist bomb in August 1979, his sense of isolation was deepened. "A mixture of desperate emotions swept over me," he wrote in his diary, "agony, disbelief, a kind of wretched numbness...I felt supremely useless and powerless."

He was a man of contradictions. Essentially kind and courteous, he was capable of rounding unfairly on a junior secretary for a trivial mistake. Despite exchanging silly jokes with Harry Secombe and Spike Milligan, not because it was expected of him but because he enjoyed it, he was a serious man, counselled by Laurens van der Post to explore the deeper spiritual values of man and nature. He loved all animals, but shot, fished, stalked and hunted them. He would take time off to explore deserts and other people's gardens, including Sissinghurst. His sports were polo and skiing. He disliked golf, abandoned tennis. In all, his image was an attractive one, an Action Man. Although he was not as good-looking as his father or elder son, his position and activities made him a glamorous figure, "the world's most eligible bachelor". While Camilla was never replaced in his deepest affections, he made no attempt to conceal from her or the public that other women attracted him too, and the girlfriends whom he escorted, each in turn arousing intense speculation, were discarded one by one with surprising ease. He was popular because he was seen to make interesting and agreeable use of his advantages, and he did not shirk his duties. But as time passed and he entered his thirties, speculation about his intentions turned into concern. Would he marry at all? Or would he, like his great-uncle David, suddenly confront the world with an unacceptable Queen?

The familiar story of Diana Spencer must in part be retold, for it had a profound influence on the monarchy. She was born in 1961, the third daughter of Viscount Althorp, who became the eighth Earl Spencer of Althorp, the family's beautiful country house in Northamptonshire. As a teenager Diana was gawky, slightly plump, and nobody, least of all her younger brother Charles, thought her likely to develop the enchanting looks that were to become the wonder of the world. Her childhood was not entirely happy. Her father divorced her much-loved mother, and married a woman whom his children much disliked, Raine Dartmouth, who took over the management and redecoration of their home. Diana's schooling was abysmal. She sat for five subjects at O-level, and failed them all. "I wasn't good at anything," she said to her biographer Andrew Morton. "I felt hopeless, a drop-out."

However, she wasn't dumb, listless or without ambition. She enjoyed pop music, clothes, dancing and diving (she had beautiful legs), but country pursuits, strange for a girl brought up on a large and beautiful estate, meant little to her. By all contemporary accounts she was a fantasist, imagining a glorious future for herself in the higher aristocracy, but for a time her aspirations rose no higher than a duchess, for which she was nicknamed 'Duch' by the family. Already her family had connections with royalty. Their home, before they moved to Althorp in 1975, was less than half a mile from Sandringham, and Diana was often taken there as a companion for Prince Andrew. Her elder sister Sarah married Robert Fellowes, son of the Sandringham land agent, and Robert became Private Secretary to the Queen.

Prince Charles first met Diana when she was seventeen, and slowly they formed a friendship. He took her to Balmoral, Cowes and Highgrove, the house he had bought in the Cotswolds. Gossip began to circulate. Then, on 6 February 1981, he proposed to her at Windsor Castle. Through an intermediary she told Andrew Morton how the proposal was offered and received:

> "He said, 'Will you marry me?' and I laughed. I remember thinking, 'This is a joke.' And I said, 'Yeah, okay,' and laughed. He was deadly serious. He said, 'You do realise that one day you will be Queen.' And a voice said to me, inside, 'You won't be Queen, but you'll have a tough role.' So I thought, 'Okay,' so I said, 'Yes.' I said, 'I love you so much, I love you so much.' He said, 'Whatever love means.' He said it then. So I thought that was great! I thought he meant that! And so he ran upstairs and rang his mother."

What are we to make of this extraordinary avowal? Diana was not a likely choice. She was nineteen, he thirty-two. She was almost totally uneducated, and had a low opinion of herself. How would she carry on a conversation at dinner with statesmen like Giscard d'Estaing? She did not share Charles's love of country sports. She was a town girl. Friends wondered what they had in common. To some biographers it seemed in retrospect, "a marriage of convenience disguised to everybody, including themselves, as a love match" (Pimlott). "She felt trapped and frightened" (Dimbleby). "A calculated act." (Bradford). "Marriage in his eyes was primarily the discharge of an obligation to his family and the nation" (Morton).

He needed someone to produce a future king, and she liked the idea of being Princess of Wales. Both were aware that his heart was committed to Camilla, and Diana was prepared to risk it. It was an "arranged" marriage, but arranged by him. Both had misgivings, he whether he loved her enough, she whether he loved her at all. In her eyes he was a sad, lonely man who needed a loving wife, and she was "hopelessly, utterly besotted with him" (Morton). They were taking a risk in taking each other, but when their engagement was announced, there was no room for second thoughts. The public were ecstatic with relief and pleasure. There was more joy in the streets than in the palaces. His family, including his mother, doubted the wisdom of it.

Diana endured the Press attention with grace and good humour. She was working in a London kindergarten where she was pursued by photographers on arrival and departure every day, answering with a smile shouted questions like, "Who's making your wedding-dress?" and "Do you hunt?" as she bent down to unlock her car. She quickly learnt how to handle herself and the public, but in private things were going from bad to worse. She found a bracelet that he was about to give to Camilla as a leaving present, engraved with the initials "GF", standing for Gladys and Fred, their nicknames for other. Sarah Bradford recalls a more memorable insult, when he danced only once with Diana and all the time with Camilla at a pre-wedding ball. Could he have been so cruel? Diana felt the strain and humiliation so keenly that only a day or two before the wedding she confided to friends that she did not think she could go through with it. "Bad luck, Duch," they replied. "Your face is on the tea towels, so you're too late to chicken out."

The wedding, on 29 July 1981, was in St Paul's. It was a sumptuous affair, and for the crowds immensely enjoyable. Diana was beautiful at last, "clothed in white samite, mystic, wonderful". As she walked back down the nave with her husband, having walked up it with her old father whom she supported more than he supported her, she caught sight of Camilla Parker Bowles in the congregation. The two women looked at each other, not, one imagines, with triumph on one side and envy on the other, but with shared consternation. The journey back to the Palace in an open-top carriage was so great a celebration of what marriage should be that Diana could not help but be affected by the euphoria she generated. The Prince felt this too, more articulately. He wrote to a friend, "It was one of the most moving experiences I have ever known ... A revelation to find the real heart and soul of the nation being exposed for a moment in good, old-fashioned, innocent enjoyment." On the balcony of Buckingham Palace he kissed his bride to the cheers of thousands.

After spending two days at Broadlands, the couple flew to Gibraltar to embark on *Britannia* for a honeymoon cruise to the Greek islands. It sounds idyllic, and as such it was reported in the British Press, but there were strains aboard. The Prince immersed himself in the novels of van der Post, encouraging Diana to read them too, but she was sick with bulimia, and he seemed to her aloof. Although he was adept at simulating marital enthusiasm in public, he scarcely bothered in private. When they returned to Balmoral, the marriage was already showing signs of strain. She refused to believe his protestations that all was over between him and Camilla. He scolded her for her jealousy. She began to dislike the man she loved, and complained to a friend of the emptiness of her life, her loss of freedom and the "heartlessness" of her husband. Although she was the idol of the crowds, she felt, in Dimbleby's words, "excluded and bewildered". There was a fundamental difference of temperament between them. She thought she had no role except to be a mother. There was much self-pity in her attitude. "Nobody has ever said to me, 'Well done,'" she complained to Morton, when she was subject to increasing adulation from the crowds. She enjoyed their attention. She even allowed herself to be photographed in a bikini when she was pregnant with William.

Her popularity became an embarrassment. On their Australian tour the crowds wanted her, not him. She was expected to walk in his shadow, but found him walking in hers. Charles minded this. Like most men, he was impatient with women's grievances, and found Diana dull in private and uninterested in any public event that did not concern her, like the Falklands War. She took no pleasure in the garden he was creating at Highgrove. "I wish you were like Fergie, all jolly," he once said to her, referring to his harum-scarum sister-in-law. Then she overheard him talking on his mobile phone to Camilla while he was having a bath. "Whatever happens," he was saying to her, "I will always love you."

Slowly she began to assert herself in ways that delighted the public but annoyed the Palace. She appeared on the stage at Covent Garden dancing with the ballet star Wayne Sleep, having rehearsed with him at Kensington Palace, and the photograph, one of the loveliest ever taken of her, appeared on the front cover of *Time*. They took eight curtain calls. Charles, who was in the audience but had had no warning of her intention, privately expressed his strong disapproval of a performance so audacious and undignified. Then Diana began to develop the interests that were to make her famous, her concern for the homeless, drug addicts, the weak and the sick. In 1991 her friend Adrian Ward-Jackson, a Governor of the Royal Ballet, was dying of Aids. For six months she visited him regularly, once taking her sons with her. She was at Balmoral when she heard that the end was near, and drove to London with a detective all through the night, arriving at the hospital at 4 a.m., and stayed with him until he died. People do not do that sort of thing to win credit. They do it because they care.

The failure of the marriage of so prominent a couple was bound to become public knowledge, and it came about in a particularly distressing way, by gossip, leaks, betrayals and ultimately by televised interviews with each of them in turn. The leaks were particularly humiliating to them both. In 1992, the Queen's *annus horribilis*, the *Sun* published the 'Squidgy tapes', the transcript of a telephone conversation, illegally recorded, between Diana and James Gilbey, a car salesman whom she had befriended. She talked to him about her unhappy life, referring to her in-laws as "this fucking family". This was followed a few months later by the publication in the *Mirror* of the "Camillagate tape", when Charles was heard to say to his mistress, "Your great achievement is to love me," and to lace his conversation with indecencies and other infelicities. Few marriages could survive such exposure. Then came the books and the broadcasts. In June 1992 Andrew Morton serialised in the *Sunday Times*, and then published as a book, *Diana, Her True Story*. It was obviously authorised by her, although it was not revealed until after her death that she had taped long interviews with an intermediary who passed them to Morton with her permission. She was obliged to deny that she was the source for the extraordinary revelations that the book contained — her jealousy of Camilla, her attempts at suicide, her bulimia.

Prince Charles answered her two years later with Jonathan Dimbleby's biography, based upon his diaries and letters, and much interrogation. He blamed his parents for what he saw as his inadequate upbringing. His mother, he said, had been remote, his father a bully. Both of them had been "unable or unwilling to proffer...the affection and appreciation" which he craved. Of his marriage he allowed Dimbleby to write, "She remained desperately unhappy, insisting on his total attention, and apparently unable to respond to his attempts to make good the damage that their mutual isolation had inflicted."

Finally, the broadcasts, in which they put their case to the world. First, Charles. In June 1994 he set aside advice, including Camilla's, to maintain a dignified silence. Having spoken about his public duties, he was asked by Dimbleby, "Did you try to be faithful in your marriage?" He replied, "Yes, until the marriage had irretrievably broken down." It was an admission of adultery, and there was no doubt that his partner was Camilla, whom he described as "a dear friend". Diana answered him in November 1995 in an hour-long interview on BBC's *Panorama*, which was watched by 23 million at home and many millions abroad. Her mistake was to wear heavy eye make-up, which gave her the appearance more of a discarded mistress than a wronged wife. She matched Charles's confession of adultery by admitting her own with James Hewitt, an army officer who had taught her sons to ride. Of herself she said, "I would like to be Queen of people's hearts."

This was too much for the real Queen. She wrote separately to her son and the Princess that she thought an early divorce was inevitable and desirable. It came about in August of the next year. Father and mother were given equal custody of the two boys, and Diana received a lump sum of about £15 million and a suite of rooms in Kensington Palace. In November 1996 she was deprived of the title Royal Highness, and her name was omitted from the roll of royalties for whom we pray every Sunday. Diana did not much mind. It would be easier for her in her new life if she were not too closely associated with the royal family, whose motive was to distance her from themselves. When they separated in 1992, the Prime Minister, John Major, had announced that "there is no reason why the Princess of Wales should not be crowned Queen in due course". That had puzzled people. Now it was clear – she was on her own.

From these extraordinary events Diana came out more

creditably than her husband, but Prince Charles slowly re-established himself in people's affections because he was seen to interest himself in problems that his predecessors had ignored, and to express himself endearingly, if strangely, like this, "I have always longed to heal things – the soil, the landscape, people and the soul." No royal had ever spoken like that before. Legends began to accumulate around him – how he would talk to growing plants, how he preferred to spend weeks at a time on a Hebridean croft, his advocacy of organic farming and alternative medicine, and most famously of all, his speech to the Royal Institute of British Architects, when he denounced the tendency to design buildings to impress other architects, not their clients, whose preference was for traditional designs, with courtyards, arches, porches and gardens. Then came the hammer blow:

> Instead of designing an extension to the elegant façade of the National Gallery which complements it and continues the concept of columns and domes, it looks as though we may be presented with a kind of vast municipal fire-station complete with the sort of tower that contains the siren. ... What is proposed is a monstrous carbuncle on the face of a much-loved and elegant friend.

He spoke for the inarticulate majority. They shared his taste for the sort of neoclassical architecture to which he gave expression in his model village, Poundbury, near Dorchester. But he lacked the capacity for the intellectual role to which he aspired. His language was unpolished, student-like, as when he wrote to John Betjeman, the Poet Laureate, inviting him to write a poem for the Queen's Silver Jubilee, "I would be enormously grateful, personally, if you felt able to conjure up your muse." People came to recognise his unusual character, his simplicity, his moral courage, and far from pitying him for having to wait so long in the wings, realised that a Prince of Wales could do things, say things, that he could never do or say as King. A good example is the Prince's Trust, which aimed to find work for young people who had fallen out of the mainstream – those who had been in trouble with the law, drug addicts, the disabled, ethnic minorities. All this he took seriously, and people noticed it to his credit.

The Queen found herself overshadowed by her children. She carried on with her customary routines, dutifully, unprovocatively, and seemingly aloof from the turmoil of their lives. By nature undemonstrative in her affections, she found it difficult to adjust her manner to their maturity. She did not wish to interfere, and so was judged indifferent. She visited Highgrove only twice in fourteen years, and let her opinion of Charles's conduct be known to him more by her silences than by her advice. As her own conduct was irreproachable, the antithesis became inevitable, "Good mother, bad children."

In 1992 the BBC broadcast another documentary about her called *Elizabeth R.* The title was astutely chosen. It was less cosy than *Royal Family* (1969), which had focused on her happy family life, which in the interval had become less than happy. It set out to explain what the Queen did, and how she handled formal and awkward situations. Boldly she agreed to speak much of the commentary herself, by the voice-over process. Thus, in talking of her audiences with her Ministers, she says, "They unburden themselves – tell one what is going on – sometimes one can help – one's a sort of sponge." When she is shown opening letters from the public, she says, "Being rather remote, it gives one an idea of what is worrying people … There is a feeling that the buck stops here," which it doesn't, because she can always pass the buck to someone else, a secretary or a government department. We see the Queen abroad, meeting

Nelson Mandela after his release from prison, addressing the US Congress, and we see her at home, at the Derby, having her portrait painted once again, and entertaining foreign statesmen. "You can do a lot if you are properly trained," she says. She appears at ease, a bit detached ("one" or "you" not "I"), capable of hard work and relaxed enjoyment. It is a pleasant portrait, and did much to reassure people that she was still the same person, stable, reliable, as she had always been. Prince Philip was given only a walk-on part.

She had reason to complain of her children. They were doing the monarchy an injury by behaving as young people are apt to behave. Her own sister had shown the way by her divorce and carefree lifestyle. Then three of her four children were also divorced – Charles from Diana, Anne from Mark Phillips, Andrew from Sarah Ferguson – and their conduct, which in an ordinary family would be regarded as high-spirited and enterprising, was considered highly improper in members of the royal family. It was difficult for them to know how far they were bound by protocol and how far they were liberated. A good example was Prince Edward's promotion of a royal version of the popular television game *It's a Knockout*, in which young people undergo a series of athletic and jocular tests of their prowess. Edward persuaded Andrew, Anne and Fergie to demonstrate that royals could enjoy themselves too. The Queen, unwisely, gave her consent. It was a disaster. They acted their parts with gusto. It was all jolly good fun. But that was not how it was received. They lacked the necessary wit to carry it off. The television audience were shocked. "Inappropriate" was the least derogatory term applied to their performance. The young royals did not know what they had done wrong. People were always clamouring for a "modern" monarchy, and when they got it, they didn't like it.

Princess Anne was admired for her horsemanship (European champion of three-day eventing at the age of twenty-one), and then for her work as President of the Save the Children Fund. But she disliked the Press, and snapped angrily at photographers who were doing a legitimate job. The *Washington Post* dubbed her "the royal sourpuss" and called her "sullen, ungracious and plain bored". But she was worth more than that. She was no snob. Her second husband, Timothy Laurence, whom she married in Scotland to avoid Church of England taboos against the remarriage of divorced persons, withdrew from public attention almost to the point of invisibility. Sarah Ferguson, on the other hand, with her colourful past and barmaid looks, was at first acclaimed as a breath of fresh air, and it was only when the *Mirror* published compromising photographs of her with John Bryan, her "financial adviser", that she was squeezed out of the royal circle. She was exuberant, careless of the impression she made, unlike her husband Andrew, Duke of York. Edward, the brightest of a mixed bunch, opted out of the Royal Marines for a career in the theatre. These royal children were not unadventurous.

Diana remained the star after her divorce. She in her thirties, and the Queen Mother in her nineties, restored whatever public affection the family had lost. Diana's position was anomalous. No longer a Royal Highness, she was still Diana, Princess of Wales, and mother of an heir to the throne. She used her freedom more profitably than she had used her marriage. It was not her nature to withdraw from public life. She invited attention, though she often complained of it, and she enjoyed the flattery, particularly in the United States, where she was the best known and most loved of our royals, though she was no longer royal. When she visited Australia in 1996, at the same time as the Queen was on a State visit to Thailand and the Prince of Wales was touring the Ukraine, Diana attracted by far the larger posse of newsmen. To Andrew Morton's interlocutor she confessed, "I don't like the glamorous occasions any more. I feel uncomfortable with them. I would much rather be doing something with sick people." She did both. I once sat opposite her at a dinner party in Spencer House, formerly her family's London home, when she was the only woman present, since it was a men's dining club. She sat undaunted between Lord Rothschild and Neil MacGregor, Director of the National Gallery, and I was struck by her vivacity, her easy conversation, her impulsiveness, her enjoyment of the occasion, and, of course, her beauty.

She was not a person who wished to hide. Nor was her desire to help the distressed in any way false. She did things few other women would care to do, embracing victims of leprosy and Aids, walking over ground only recently cleared of landmines, cuddling limbless black babies in the African sun. It was the alternation of the good-time girl and the angel of mercy, of dignity and escapades, and her evident love for her children, that won people's admiration and gave her new confidence, a purpose in life. But it was not easy to combine her roles. She enjoyed being a celebrity, but also wanted to be someone who could shop alone in Bond Street. She was not ashamed of her love affairs – it is usual for young people to form new relationships after a divorce – but, within limits, she tried to keep them private.

Then she died, after midnight on 31 August 1997, in a Paris underpass. Her car, driven by an inebriated driver and pursued by the paparazzi, went out of control and crashed into a pillar. The driver, and Diana's lover, Dodi Al Fayed, who was sitting beside her, were killed instantly. Diana never recovered consciousness, and died in a Paris hospital a few hours later.

The people's reaction was extraordinary. She was *their* Princess, as Tony Blair instantly named her, implying that she was different from other royals and the only one who was any good. The flowers that were strewn outside Kensington and Buckingham Palaces were gestures of inconsolable grief. British reserve – as at Mafeking, VE Day, the 1966 World Cup victory – was cast aside. Grief fed on other people's grief. When books of condolence were opened at St James's Palace, people queued for up to eleven hours to sign them and add the words of gratitude that they had been composing during their long wait. Of the mourners, 70 per cent, it was said, were under forty.

The royal family were on holiday at Balmoral. As soon as the news reached them, Prince Charles flew to Paris and returned to London with the coffin. But where was the Queen? It was noticed with scorn that at the morning service at Crathie church, the vicar delivered his prepared sermon, with jokes that seemed cruelly out of place. Public indignation focused on one symbol, the bare flagpole on Buckingham Palace. Why was there no flag at half-mast? At Balmoral, too, the Royal Standard flew to its full height. It was hastily explained that the royal flag was never flown at half-mast even for the death of a king, and that it was customary to fly the standard at Balmoral when the Queen was in residence. These reasons were thought to be insensitive excuses. The Queen must show she cared. Something more was required than an expression of regret from Balmoral. The Queen must come south. There was some sympathy for the idea that the two young Princes, who were also at Balmoral, should be allowed time to recover from the shock of their mother's death away from the gaze of the crowds. But the family's remoteness, both in space and emotional detachment, as if they were thinking "What's all this fuss about?", was unacceptable. It was the only time in her reign that the Queen found herself unpopular. The people needed her presence in London, where Diana's body lay, not because she was her mother-in-law

but because it was an occasion of profound national significance, and she was head of state. This, at any rate, is what
the tabloids said, and the tabloids for once did not dictate
but echoed what the people thought.

So the family flew south, and the flag was lowered to
half-mast. The courtiers feared a hostile demonstration in
London. As the Queen left her car at the Palace gates to
examine some of the floral tributes, there was silence in the
crowd. Then a girl of eleven stepped forward with a bunch
of five red roses. "Would you like me to place them there
for you?" asked the Queen gently. "No, Your Majesty,
they are for you." The crowd began to clap. The little girl,
did she but realise it, had saved the day. That evening the
Queen spoke on television to express on behalf of the
nation the profound sorrow that she shared with them. Her
speech had been written for her by Sir Robert Fellowes,
and she read it through, twice, before she went, live, on
air. He asked her (as Alan Lascelles had asked her, just fifty
years before in South Africa), "Can you say this and believe
it?" "Yes," she replied, "I can believe it very clearly." She
spoke of Diana as "an exceptional and gifted human
being". She did not say she loved her, but acknowledged
that there were "lessons to be drawn from her life" and
from "the extraordinary and moving reaction to her
death". Then she added, "I share in your determination to
cherish her memory." It was enough.

The Queen agreed that Diana must have a royal funeral.
It was not a State funeral, which is reserved for Monarchs
and an exceptional commoner like Winston Churchill, but
it was regarded as such. The long, slow procession of the
gun carriage from Kensington Palace, and the service in
Westminster Abbey, were watched by thousands in the
streets and billions on television around the world. The
crowds came, as one woman expressed it, "because I want
to be part of the love", and a Dutch visitor who happened

to be in London said, "There is only one woman in the world worthy of such a funeral," and she was not thinking of Mother Teresa, who died in the same week.

The two Princes, walking behind the coffin with their father, grandfather and uncle, lent the occasion both pathos and dignity. The crowd's mood was sombre, but also faintly bitter. They had lost her, and in a curious way felt guilty for her death, angry with the media for persecuting her and with the royal family for deserting her. Elton John's emotional rendering of "Candle in the Wind" set the royals apart from the vast crowds of young people listening and watching in the parks. Diana's brother, Earl Spencer, caught their mood when he declared, in the Queen's presence, "She needed no royal title to generate her particular brand of magic," and claimed the two boys, William and Harry, as his own family, and stated he would care for them. It was a gratuitous insult to the Queen, and the most damaging consequence was immediate. The cheers that his address evoked outside the Abbey were taken up inside. The young Princes were seen to join in the applause, but not the Queen or the Duke of Edinburgh. Spencer had expressed the people's desire for a different monarchy, one which Diana had symbolised by blending the royal concept of duty with the humane concept of romance. She had done more to alter the traditional role of monarchy by her death than she had in life, or so it seemed at the moment when her coffin, laden with flung flowers, was driven through London's northern suburbs to Althorp, and buried on a lake-island where nobody could approach her.

## IX

O F course, the reaction was unfair to the Queen and the Prince of Wales. William and Harry did not turn to their uncle for consolation and advice, but to their father. Diana had not known how to quell the Press attention she deliberately aroused. She should have realised that publicity means scrutiny, and scrutiny involves exposure. She could be exasperating. She might have chosen a worthier lover than the one who died with her. What sort of Queen would she have made? Would she have tolerated the tedium of royal routines with the patience of Elizabeth II? Did Diana, in fact, deserve so flattering an obsequy? Was she worthy of the tribute which a woman attached to a memorial bouquet five years after her death: "There is only one Queen that will ever be known by the people of England"?

Gradually the royals recovered their reputations, and Diana's death did not, as is often claimed, greatly affect their behaviour. They carried on as before. Prince Charles wisely took his sons to South Africa soon after her funeral, and showed them in the gentlest way how to treat significant people like Nelson Mandela and please the insignificant. The Press, seeing that he was a good father, treated him more kindly. His views on agriculture, horticulture, architecture and medicine were no longer mocked. He took the trouble to find out things which another royal would wait to be told, and then forget. He would send for experts on foot-and-mouth or GM crops whose articles he had read in learned journals, and interrogate them. He gave weekend parties at Sandringham for fifteen guests, few of whom he had met before but wanted to meet, and they came because they wanted to meet him. When the Queen Mother died, his impromptu television tribute to her was the most moving of all, and his evident distress at her funeral made it clear to everyone that a man capable of such love for a grandmother must be a man of unusual sensibility. But there was still the problem of Camilla. Her good taste and reticence slowly won people's interest, and then their affection. The Queen Mother had resolutely opposed their marriage, but now that both she and Diana were dead, things could be different.

Princess Margaret died five years after Diana, and a few months before her mother. She had become despondent about the lack of direction in her life. She never identified herself, like Anne and Diana, with any newsworthy cause, and the tabloids treated her brutally because she had no respect for them. She enjoyed private more than public occasions, and made no effort to conceal her preference. She was said to drink too much, smoke too much, spend too much, and her love affairs aroused more scandal than amusement. All this tended to obscure her good points, that she carried out some 300 public engagements a year, was deeply religious, a wonderful mother (taking her children to see just *one* beautiful object in a museum, and look closely at just *one* beautiful building) and was seriously interested in the arts, the favourite royal of people like John Betjeman and Lucian Freud. But in her declining years her popularity faded. For the public she became a disappointed old woman in a wheelchair. When she died in February 2002, few bouquets were laid at the gates of Kensington Palace. Six years after Diana's death a ring of bright water, the size of a football field, was proposed in her memory in Hyde Park. For Princess Margaret there was only a plaque in a side chapel of St George's, Windsor.

It was quite different for the Queen Mother. Three times her life had taken a dramatic twist – commoner to royal, minor royal to Queen, widowed Queen to Queen Mother – and she handled each change superbly, particularly the last. She had never been beautiful, but her face was pleasing. She had no dress sense. Her appearance in middle age was described by an American journalist as "more like a retired actress than a Queen". That did not matter. She grew old in a way that every woman envied. She never acted like a dowager. She was reticent, but not aloof. She was always willing to perform small ceremonies – opening a bridge, giving away prizes, leading a winner into the ring – and she never apologised for her extravagances. She was one of the few celebrities whose reputation told the whole truth about her. When she died on 30 March 2002 people said that it was just like her to live for over a hundred years. Though she was in part an adventuress, she also represented stability. She embodied the traditional values of the nation, but with zest, and refurbished the royal style.

The problem remained what to do with the minor royals, and to define how minor they are. It would be reasonable to conclude that those entitled to His/Her Royal Highness are royal, and those without are not. But while neither of the Princess Royal's two children, Peter and Zara, are HRH, Prince Andrew's two, Beatrice and Eugenie, are, because they are fifth and sixth in succession to the throne, and their first cousins, being children of a daughter, are only ninth and tenth. Some of the more prominent royals, like the seventh Earl of Harewood, grandson of King George V, are scarcely regarded as royal at all. In general, the nearer to the throne they are, the more duties they are required to perform and the more public attention they attract.

Lower down the scale, where dukes and duchesses become simple Windsors, attention focuses on the girls if they are pretty and on the boys if they are bad. Most manage to escape the dilemma by being half-royal, like Viscount Linley (not HRH) who founded and runs a very successful furniture-making business in Chelsea, and Prince Michael of Kent (HRH) who has been much abused by the Press for paying a rent of only £60 a week for a Kensington Palace flat, but is a most conscientious, worthy man, and carries out 170 public duties a year in addition to running his own consultancy firm. When the minor royals appear on the Buckingham Palace balcony as a family group, nobody is quite certain who is who, though they notice that Fergie is missing, in spite of her resumed cohabitation with her divorced husband, the Duke of York. There are too many of them, and yet too few, for royals are in great demand for charity and other functions, where their presence sets a seal of approval on the event. Katharine, Duchess of Kent, for example, was born a commoner and is the most unroyal of royals, but does them great credit, as I found when she attended the 500th anniversary of the foundation of my local grammar school. She has the gift of pleasing by doing the unexpected, like picking out a single child from the crowd, and asking for a second helping of raspberry fool. These functions are not anachronistic or snobbish. They give innocent pleasure to a vast number of people. The problem is whether these juniors, like their seniors, should be spared the burden of earning their living while carrying out royal duties with perks but no pay.

Let me cite, for example, the notorious case of Edward, the Queen's third son, who was created Earl of Wessex when he married Sophie Rhys-Jones in 1999. They were a likeable couple, he active in the theatrical world, and she an attractive blonde, often mistaken for Diana herself. In 1993 Edward had launched Ardent Productions, a documentary television company, promising not to trade on his royal connections. Three months after their wedding,

Sophie, now Countess of Wessex, was accused of exploiting her royal status by having herself photographed promoting Rover cars at the Frankfurt Motor Show. Rover was a client of R-J.H Public Relations, of which she was a director. Her action seemed to the public a minor transgression. The argument went, "They cannot shed the glamour of their names. Why should it be considered disgraceful if they make use of them, when professional people do so all the time?"

Then came the scandal of the *News of the World*. Sophie gave an interview to a man disguised as a sheik, but actually a reporter from the newspaper. Hoping to engage the "Sheik" as a client for her PR company, she made several indiscreet remarks, describing Cherie Blair as "horrid, horrid, horrid", William Hague, then Leader of the Opposition, as "deformed", and the Queen as "the old dear". She predicted that Charles and Camilla ("number one on the unpopular people list") would marry soon after the "old lady" (the Queen Mother) died. Her business partner told the fake Sheik that her royal connections raised the profile of their clients. Americans would never refuse an invitation from a royal countess, while they might if it came from Ms Sophie Rhys-Jones. The conversation was taped and, as soon as the deceit was discovered, an attempt was made to persuade the newspaper to surrender the tape in exchange for a personal interview. In the event the *News of the World* published the tape in full, "to clear the air". The public blamed Sophie for her indiscretions more than the newspaper for its perfidy. Meanwhile the Earl of Wessex persuaded the Sultan of Brunei, the world's richest man, to invest £200,000 in Ardent, on condition that the company included the Sultan's own garden in their "royal gardens" film.

The Wessex pair were already in trouble because they were living too grandly for a couple whose finances were rocky. Ardent was losing money. They were inhabiting a fifty-seven-room mansion, Bagshot Park, with the servants and security needed to run such a large establishment. Worse was to follow. Ardent Productions was accused of filming Prince William when he arrived for his first term at St Andrew's University, after the other film companies, by agreement, had departed. The Queen was not pleased. She was giving Edward £141,000 a year from her own purse and did not expect him to disgrace her family. Under pressure, the Earl and Countess announced that they would give up their commercial careers to become whole-time royals, and the Queen agreed to increase Edward's allowance to £249,000, the same as her annual donation to the Duke of York. The whole incident was faintly discreditable, and it raised once more the question of how royalty could be combined with business. The public were ambivalent. They wanted active young royals to "do a proper job" and earn their keep, but at the same time attend to their royal duties. They must not exploit their royal status for commercial profit. They must look the part, but not live too grandly. They must keep their royal and business lives separate, and they must not be a burden on the public funds. The public hardly knew what they meant. They were asking the impossible.

The Queen took up her duties in time-honoured fashion, and by conducting them without noticeable post-Diana change, reminded the nation of the most important contribution that monarchy can make – continuity, stability and grace. There were the big annual events – the Trooping, the Opening of Parliament, Armistice Day, the garden parties and investitures – to which were added special ceremonies – a wedding, a funeral, a road or building to be declared open, a new museum, a festival, a Dome. These were the public events. The Court Circular, which few newspapers printed and few readers read, recorded them all, including the semi-private functions, visiting hospitals, schools and homes for the elderly, receiving ambassadors, British and foreign, who must be greeted on appointment and thanked on departure.

Few people are privileged to witness such formalities, and it is rarely that we are allowed a glimpse of them. An exceptional account was written by Raymond Seitz, American ambassador to the Court of St James's from 1991 to 1994, one of the best-liked, most anglophile, wittiest of them all. In his book *Over Here* he described the scene when he presented his credentials. He was nervous. For him it was a unique occasion, for which nobody can be adequately briefed. For the Queen it was a 2000th repetition. She had an advantage:

> I was positioned in front of a stratosphere double-door [wrote Seitz]. Looking as relaxed as possible, I went over in my mind the little minuet I would have to dance – was it two steps forward and one bow, or two bows and one step? Do not offer your hand unless she offers hers first. Do not ask any personal questions, such as "How are the kids?".
>
> At a signal, the doors swung open. In the middle of a cavernous, golden reception room, at a distance roughly the same as Chicago to Minneapolis, stood the Queen. She wore a simple day-dress – no sceptre or crown, no diamonds, and not a throne or a jester in sight – and a little handbag dangled from her wrist. Bow, two steps. Stop. Bow again. Stride across the infinite field of carpet. Stop. Bow. "I have the honour, Your Majesty, to present the letter of recall of my predecessor and my letter of credential." I knew my lips were moving, but I wasn't certain any words were coming out.
>
> We then began a brief conversation ... She asked for my opinion about the Soviet Union, and I said I thought it was falling apart. Her questions were direct, but her

voice seemed oddly tentative, and while she listened to the replies, she did so with an eye that drifted to the middle distance.

Her presence adds importance to any occasion. To be appointed ambassador to Great Britain is an undoubted honour, especially for a career diplomatist like Raymond Seitz, but to confirm it in so strange a manner is something that only a Monarch can perform. The elaborate stage-management of the little ceremony is intended to be slightly awesome to everyone but her. Seitz recounted the incident with humour, but he did not think it absurd.

He also gives us an idea of the Queen's attitude on such occasions. She is determined that the ceremony be performed without error on either side, but having done it so often, she is not particularly interested. No refreshments are offered, no hope expressed for future meetings, no enquiries after his kids (though he was allowed to present his wife). It is soon over. She is strong and can be quite formidable, and reveals little of her intelligence and imagination. But she is alert all the time.

If she had not been born royal, she would have been regarded as a clever, likeable woman with conventional habits and beliefs, a Conservative, a good wife and mother, lacking in vanity and ambition. Being royal has not made a great difference to her, except to make her more cautious and slightly distant. She has an inborn resistance to change. She hopes that problems will sort themselves out, and while she responds to new ideas, she does not often initiate them. She is not out of date. She visits newspaper offices, pubs and a rehearsal of *Oklahoma!* She can operate a computer, has a royal website, watches television for the racing and, one likes to suppose, for the insight the soap operas afford into other people's lives. It is difficult to imagine her reading a biography of herself, because she already knows all the facts, has seen all the pictures, and is not particularly interested in the comments.

She is not so much at ease in public as Diana was. There is a famous photograph taken of her in a Glasgow bungalow where she sits upright at a tea table, a cut-out figure, confronting the tenant-widow, victim of a stroke, who has laid the table with cups and a plate of sandwiches. Nobody is happy. The sandwiches remain untasted. The Queen feels awkward, hating to be photographed in this situation, knowing that she is not good at handling the unfamiliar. Once in Australia, a little schoolboy asked her a question which she had never expected to be asked in all her life: "Who are you?" She stared at him uncomprehending and walked away. Diana would have gathered him into her arms. Then there was a well-remembered incident at the opening of the Greenwich Dome at midnight on 31 December 1999. It was thought appropriate for the vast audience to sing "Auld Lang Syne". Tony Blair extended a crossed hand to the Queen who was standing next to him. Tentatively she allowed him to take her hand, but queens do not cross them even with prime ministers. Her studied aloofness did not enliven the occasion. An elderly face in repose looks glummer than its wearer feels, and it is the penalty of fame that in public she is always on camera. She cannot keep smiling all the time.

Few things are a treat for her because everyone is watching to see how much she is enjoying the treat. Every chance word will be repeated. She can ask safe questions ("Where do you live?" "Where did you get that lovely hat?") but must avoid risky ones ("What did you have for lunch today?" "Where is your husband?"), so she appears duller than she is. When unengaged, she will sometimes attend a private dinner party, arriving last, leaving first, but even then she cannot rely on not being reported. It is a shackled life. She must long for the privacy of Sandringham and Balmoral.

At a Guildhall lunch to celebrate their Golden Wedding, the Duke of Edinburgh said of his wife, "People in her position have to learn to accept certain constraints – but they also discover that it gives them exceptional opportunities." What could he mean by "opportunities"? She can certainly give a great deal of pleasure to a great many people. But politically her opportunities are rare. She has no influence on home affairs, even those that concern her closely, like the reform of the House of Lords. On foreign affairs her influence is greater, by her treatment of eminent visitors from abroad and her special relationship with the Commonwealth. Ben Pimlott puts it succinctly: "She had achieved the remarkable feat of retaining the loyalty and sentimental attachment of the leaders of member states, even when they had been bitterly opposed to United Kingdom policies."

With the devolution of Wales and Scotland, both were now in a sense Commonwealth countries, though remaining part of the United Kingdom. Scotland in particular needed careful handling. Scottish MPs sat in the Westminster Parliament – indeed, both the Chancellor of the Exchequer (Gordon Brown) and Foreign Secretary (then Robin Cook) sat for Scottish constituencies – but Scotland now had its own Parliament, which it was the Queen's duty to open. Her position was delicate. A MORI poll in 1991 had revealed that a small majority desired to substitute an elected president for an English queen. On the other hand, Elizabeth was herself half-Scottish, and had two Scottish residences, Holyrood House and Balmoral. How would she be received when she travelled north to open the first Scottish Assembly in 1999 – as the Queen of Scots, or as the visiting Queen of England? Would her presence on this historic occasion be taken as a compliment to their separate nationhood or as a reproach that they were cutting themselves adrift from England? Tactfully, she played down her Englishness, played up her Scottishness. The streets of Edinburgh were lined with cheering crowds. The situation was saved by their love of pageantry and their warmth of heart.

A more difficult situation arose in 1997 on the Indian subcontinent, when the Queen visited Pakistan and India to celebrate the fiftieth anniversary of their independence. She enjoyed every luxury except anonymity. Her slightest word was analysed for *double entendre*. No bitterness was caused by memories of British rule. Both countries were now independent sovereign states and members of the Commonwealth. The Queen herself had said, "The Commonwealth bears no resemblance to the Empire of the past. It is an entirely new conception," and she was welcomed as head of a loose federation, which nobody cared to define too closely. The trouble was that neither State was on speaking terms with the other, owing to the Kashmir dispute, both claiming it as their own territory, and during the Queen's visit artillery fire was regularly exchanged across the border. Her public pronouncements required very fine tuning. She must not give the impression of favouring either side. She could speak of the welcome that Pakistani emigrants were receiving in Britain and of Diana's interest in the welfare of the poor, but when she said she hoped that the two countries would "renew their efforts to resolve their historic disagreements", meaning Kashmir, there was uproar in India. Was she suggesting that they should make concessions to Pakistan?

Robin Cook, who accompanied her, explained that her innocuous remarks (which he had probably drafted himself) only expressed a hope that the two countries might become reconciled, the sort of inoffensive platitude that the Secretary-General of the United Nations utters every day. It did no good, and when the Queen asked to meet some of India's untouchables, it was held to be a criticism of India's

Prince Charles and Lord Mountbatten. 'They formed so close an intimacy that Charles touched in his great-uncle a more tender chord, and he in Charles a capacity to make his own decisions' (p. 88).

OPPOSITE PAGE
TOP Charles and
Diana on their
wedding day. 'He
wrote to a friend,
"It was one of
the most moving
experiences I have
ever known"'
(p. 96).

OPPOSITE PAGE
BELOW Diana
dances at Covent
Garden with
Wayne Sleep. They
took eight curtain
calls. (p. 97).

In 1992 the Queen entertained her Prime Minister, John Major,
and her surviving former Prime Ministers, to celebrate the 40th
anniversary of her accession.

She rides with Nelson Mandela on his visit to London in July
1995.

She visits the Kalakshetra Foundation in Madras in 1997. 'The stress of being the centre of attention for hours on end is great' (p. 67).

The Queen in a Glasgow bungalow in 1999, 'hating to be photographed in that situation, knowing that she is not good at handling the unfamiliar'. (p. 116)

At Fredricton, New Brunswick during her Canadian Tour in October 2002.

In Ipswich during her Golden Jubilee tour of Britain in July 2002.
'The Monarchy was a feel-good factor'. (p. 122).

ABOVE Prince Charles with his mother (whom he called 'Mummy' on introducing her) and Cliff Richard at the pop concert in the Buckingham Palace garden during the Golden Jubilee.

OPPOSITE PAGE TOP 'God Save the Queen' was projected on to the Palace during the London Jubilee celebrations.

OPPOSITE PAGE BELOW 'The Queen declared that the purpose of the Jubilee was to thank us for our support, when its real purpose was for us to thank her for her forbearance' (p.122).

Prince Charles and Camilla Parker Bowles. 'We should not expose this decent woman, and this man born and worthy to be King, to the humiliation' of denying her the right to be his Queen. (p. 139).

social system. The tour was pronounced a failure. The Queen was not blamed. It is one of her advantages that she is always given the benefit of the doubt. The failure was attributed to the tactlessness of the Foreign Secretary, and Tony Blair asked the Queen to make an unprecedented statement, that she was perfectly satisfied with the arrangements and with Mr Robin Cook.

My second and more important example of the fragility of the Commonwealth, and the Queen's therapeutic role in it, is Australia. She has visited the continent many times, and watched it develop from the second most populated Dominion in the Empire into a mature and self-confident nation anxious to assert its independence. British rule, even though nominal, was seen to be increasingly anachronistic, and the Queen its symbol. She was not born Australian, nor did she have a permanent home there. There was nothing personal about Australians' change of attitude. Her visits had always been welcomed. But in the 1990s the republican movement was gaining ground. The royal divorces had done more damage to the monarchy in Australia than in England. The Prince of Wales was much criticised, and although people had not forgotten his unflinching response to a supposed attempt on his life in Sydney in 1994, King Charles III was not a sovereign to whom they looked forward with any pleasure. Princess Diana's visit to Australia in the year before she died some-what revived monarchist sentiments. They adored her, but her death, paradoxically, brought nearer the decision to drop the Queen.

A referendum was held in November 1999, and the polls forecast an easy victory for the Republicans by 80 to 90 per cent. In fact the vote was 55 per cent in favour of keeping the monarchy, largely because the choice put to the voters was between retaining the Queen as head of state and a president elected by a two-thirds majority of the Canberra

Parliament. Australians demanded the right to elect their president directly, and their only way of insisting on it was to vote for the status quo to which the big majority of them were opposed. The result was heralded as a triumph for the Queen, but she knew very well that it was no such thing. In his masterly biography, Pimlott suggests that it was open to her to accept "the implicit verdict of the poll...Such an act might have been a political master-stroke." But if she had abdicated her Antipodean sovereignty, there would have been turmoil in Australia, and the precedent would have raised the same question in every other part of the Commonwealth. Could they, too, not be freed from this anachronism?

As it was, the Queen embarked in March 2000 on her thirteenth Australian tour as if nothing unusual had happened. Her delicate position was eased by her keynote speech in Sydney, where she said, "I have always made it clear that the future of the monarchy in Australia is an issue for you, the Australian people, and for you alone to decide by democratic and constitutional means." Even more effective was her reply to a reporter who asked her to which group she had most enjoyed talking: "To the Republicans, of course." Still, the signals were unmistakable. She was not invited to declare open the Sydney Olympic Games, which raised nationalistic pride to a new level, and her portrait was discreetly removed from inside public buildings. It was assumed that Australia would eventually discard the royal connection, but with the election of a pro-Queen Prime Minister, John Howard, in November 2001, the decision was once more postponed. In England the issue was not much debated, its outcome being considered inevitable, and in conformity with Britain's decline as a world power.

## X

IT was in Australia that the Queen launched the Golden Jubilee to celebrate her fifty years on the throne. At the age of seventy-five, only three days after the cremation of her sister's body, she embarked on a round-the-world flight – London–Jamaica–New Zealand–Australia–London – knowing that at every stopping place she would be subject to the stares of millions, and that any deviation from uninterrupted smiles and waves would be taken as a sign of grumpiness, when it was only weariness. There were, as usual, political complications. A poll taken in New Zealand, shortly before her arrival, returned only 58 per cent in favour of retaining the monarchy, and the Prime Minister, Helen Clarke, declared publicly that it was but a matter of time before her country became a republic. When the Queen landed at Adelaide she was greeted by the Governor General, Peter Hollingworth, whose resignation was demanded by Opposition politicians for his alleged failure to stamp out sexual abuses among the clergy when he was Anglican Archbishop of Brisbane. Who could have foreseen that embarrassment? How could the Queen be expected to deal with it? She dismissed it with a broad smile, saying, "I don't want to hear about that." Because she was on her best behaviour, so was everyone else. With simulated delight, she showed interest in a bewildering variety of people, places, things and information. It cannot have been much fun.

There were fears, as there had been in 1977, that the

Jubilee celebrations in the United Kingdom might flop. We were grateful for the Queen's industry and goodness, but goodness, as Jan Morris said, is a hard thing to celebrate. In a *Telegraph* poll 43 per cent declared that they were not looking forward to the Jubilee at all. The public needed a jolt, said the same newspaper, to remind them that "love of the past can bring zest to the present and a sense of confidence in the future". The monarchy was a feel-good factor. The Queen declared that the purpose of the Jubilee was to thank us for our support, when its real purpose was for us to thank her for her forbearance. Cynicism about the monarchy was temporarily suspended. Public rejoicing stimulated private rejoicing. People flew the national flag from the bonnets of their cars, and children painted the St George cross on their faces. Villages held Jubilee fêtes on their greens. My own village gave an open-air tea party for 600, followed by three-legged races and a Punch and Judy. The national anthem was played to remind us what it was all about, and I made a two-minute loyal speech. The same kind of celebration was happening all over the country. Once again the Queen had given us an excuse for a party.

On the larger scale, the Jubilee was celebrated by metropolitan and regional events. The Queen visited seventy towns and cities during her two-month tour of the United Kingdom, hosted a dinner for all the reigning European Sovereigns, another for her six surviving Prime Ministers, and gave six garden parties. The metropolitan events were televised nationally, the regionals regionally. To Londoners events that happen outside London haven't happened at all. Even the review of the Fleet at Portsmouth was largely ignored by the national press, possibly because only five first-line ships were on parade, compared with the 200 at the spectacular Coronation review of 1953. We did not wish to advertise our decline. Much of the Queen's tour took place in the semi-privacy of county towns. Wherever she went, there was a tremendous turnout. Where she didn't go, like Kent and Sussex, there was jealousy.

These regional events were bound to be repetitive, and for the royal party, who had seen the best of everything, the second-best required a special effort of appreciation. Let me give one example. On 31 July the Queen visited Scunthorpe in Humberside. At the railway station (most of the tour was by the royal train) she and the Duke of Edinburgh were received by the Lord Lieutenant and the Mayor of North Lincolnshire. She drove to a hospice, where she opened a new wing. Then, unusually, she visited a mosque and was received by the Imam. Next, she walked about through the centre of Scunthorpe, still escorted by the Mayor. She lunched at Normanby Hall, a Regency mansion publicly owned. Then she left by train for Nottingham, where a similar procedure was followed. The Duke of Edinburgh did not follow in her footsteps the whole time, but sensibly detached himself to view the Art Centre where he met some young people who had earned his Award. The only curious event was when the royal couple "painted the eyes of Chinese lions", a ceremony which the Court Circular does not explain. The day had been a gala day for Scunthorpe. For the royal couple it was another duty well organised and satisfactorily performed.

The metropolitan events were on a grand scale, unspoiled by rain, rowdiness, protests or bomb scares. Contemporary rumbles of discontent in Belfast, Israel, India and Pakistan did not disturb the equanimity of the capital. The only competition came from the World Cup football matches in Japan. The Jubilee was not so much a demonstration of delight in the Queen still being Queen, as a demonstration of delight in us still being us. It was unashamedly jingoistic. At the same time it had a religious and cultural content. The golden coach was once more trundled to St Paul's. A reception was held in the Royal Academy for artists, ballet dancers, actors and writers. A special performance was staged at Covent Garden, at £1000 a seat for those inside, free on television screens for those outside. The highlights were two concerts, one classical, the other pop, in the garden of Buckingham Palace, for 12,000 in the garden itself and 40,000 watching in the Mall and the parks. A note of frivolity prevailed. The Prince of Wales, introducing his mother, began, "Your Majesty" – pause – "Mummy." The classical music was light, to suit her tastes – Kiri de Kanawa, *Figaro*, fireworks to go with Handel, and Camilla Parker Bowles to go with Prince Charles. The pop concert was hosted by Ben Elton and Dame Edna Everage, and featured Paul McCartney recreating the Beatles song "All You Need Is Love", accompanied by Lenny Henry, Shirley Bassey, Cliff Richard and the girl-band Atomic Kitten. Both audiences were equally enthusiastic, the classical audience litter-free. The following day there was a procession of 20,000 performers parading up the Mall to the Victoria memorial where the Queen sat, like her great-great-grandmother, in semi-state, while Concorde, escorted by the Red Arrows in terrifying proximity, streaked overhead.

In Edinburgh and Glasgow, where Union Jacks alternated with symbols of Scottish independence, the Queen walked about in mutual amity. She was whisked by helicopter to Stornoway in the Western Isles, to Wick in the remote north-east and to Aberdeen to attend the Scottish Parliament, which met there while their permanent home in Edinburgh was still under construction. Ten Nationalist SNP members absented themselves with polite excuses of sickness, traffic congestion and prior engagements, but this did not seem to matter.

The climax of the Jubilee were the Commonwealth

Games in Manchester, opened by the Queen in late July and closed by her in early August. Five-thousand athletes from seventy-two nations took part, and when the public wondered how there could be seventy-two competitive nations when there were only fifty-four members of the Commonwealth, it was explained that the United Kingdom was divided for the purpose into its four constituent parts, and that the old outposts of Empire like Gibraltar and Nauru (which with a population of only 11,000 won two gold medals) were awarded separate nationhood for the occasion. Zimbabwe was there, though politically in disgrace. Flags were flown, medals awarded, the gold in quantity to Australia and England, the first saluted by "Advance Australia Fair", the host country by "Land of Hope and Glory", its tune exhilarating, but the words, if anyone knew them or listened to them, oddly discordant with the reality of twenty-first-century Britain:

> Land of Hope and Glory,
> Mother of the Free,
> How shall we extol thee
> Who are born of thee?
> Wider still, and wider,
> Shall thy bounds be set.
> God who made thee mighty
> Make thee mightier yet.

The Queen, the focus of 40,000 in the stadium alone, looked puzzled but not displeased. The chief victor of the Games was Manchester itself, whose brilliant stage-management raised her fame from bronze to gold. In consequence she became a serious contender for the Olympics 2012, in spite of the downpour that nearly wrecked the closing ceremony.

The Jubilee was pronounced a success. The crowds had

been large except in Glasgow. Only two eggs were thrown, in Nottingham. The warmest welcome came in ethnically divided places like Newham in east London. Fears that interest might subside after three months proved unfounded. "The people's tribute", wrote *The Times*, "was very much directed at the Queen herself, not only for her longevity, but for her stoicism and constancy." That was true and well deserved.

## XI

A<sup>s</sup> head of the United Kingdom and the Commonwealth the Queen never permits herself to suggest that the kingdom is disunited or that the Commonwealth is fraying at the edges. She stands for national optimism. As she is known never to act except on ministerial advice, she is given little credit when things go right, and no blame when they go wrong. This particularly applies in war. The only military disaster of her reign was the Suez operation. In all the others – Korea, Vietnam, Falklands, Bosnia, Kosovo, Gulf – either Britain's contribution has been marginal, or we have won. The Crown was not involved except as nominal head of the armed services, and there was no need, as in previous wars, for the Monarch's presence in the field. When Prince Andrew flew a helicopter over the Falklands it was the only occasion when a member of the royal family was engaged in active operations during her reign. There was some criticism that none was present in the Gulf.

It has been said that the Queen has never made a mistake. She is well advised, and her natural instinct is to play safe. She might have stood more stoutly at her sister's side during the Townsend affair. She might have dismissed Anthony Blunt when she first heard of his treachery, but she retained him on the advice of MI5 who hoped to extract more information from him, impossible once he had been publicly exposed. In October 1966 she delayed a week too long her visit to the Welsh village of Aberfan, where a slag-heap collapsed on a school, killing more than a hundred children, but visits by royalty and senior politicians to scenes of a disaster require careful timing, for fear of interrupting rescue work or seeming to seek publicity for themselves. Again the situation was saved by a little girl who gave the Queen a bunch of flowers labelled "From the remaining children of Aberfan". The tabloids loved that. She cannot be blamed for appointing Lord Home to succeed Harold Macmillan as Prime Minister, though it was an eccentric choice, recommended by Macmillan himself. Finally, her immediate reaction to Princess Diana's death was less emotional than the people wanted, but this was soon remedied. The shortness of this list of "failures" is extraordinary for a reign of fifty years, and it cannot be attributed to her advice and caution alone. She uses her judgement too.

No sin has ever been imputed to the Queen. No breath of scandal has touched her, as it has her husband, sister and children. If she is not a deeply religious woman, she accepts the faith she was brought up to accept. She attends church regularly to set an example, but only on the most pious days does she take Communion. We can have no notion whether she believes literally in the Virgin Birth, the bodily resurrection of Christ and the redemption of sins, and we do not need to know. As the Supreme Governor of the Church of England her paradoxical duty is to remain silent. She is not likely to endorse Prince Charles's wish to be known as Defender of Faith not *the* Faith, since nobody is more exclusively Protestant than the Queen. Tolerant of other faiths she may be, but they are "foreign". When Prince Charles accepted an invitation from the Pope to attend an ecumenical mass at St Peter's, she vetoed the visit on the grounds that any reconciliation with Rome would jeopardise his right of succession to the throne. The oath of allegiance to the Queen, which bishops take on succeeding to a diocese, is quite specific: "I, renouncing all foreign princes and prelates [i.e. the Pope], acknowledge that I hold the said bishopric in spirituality and temporality only from Your Majesty." Nor do we know what she thinks of the ordination of women, abortion, homosexual priests – all moral dilemmas that face the Church today. She cannot give a lead in these matters.

She does not even appoint the bishops and archbishops. By a curious anomaly, the Prime Minister does, probably to her relief, since these appointments can be politically controversial, like that of her new Archbishop, Rowan Williams, who even before his enthronement at Canterbury made public his opposition to an invasion of Iraq without United Nations approval. Perhaps her steadfast faith may come into conflict with the Church's attempts to compromise with growing secularisation. It is said that a third of the Anglican clergy privately doubt the doctrines, but not the ethics, which they propound weekly from the pulpit. They stand for "a credible faith for reasonable people". The Queen is known to prefer the King James Bible and the Book of Common Prayer to any modern version, and finds it difficult to come to terms with illegitimacy and divorce, gay rights and apostasy. Her Christmas messages proclaim the traditional view of God as just and merciful, whatever the evidence to the contrary, and although she is well aware that many of her people are not Christians at all, she believes in the Establishment of the Church of England and that the Crown's imprimatur is an important factor in its survival. Her relations with the archbishops are analogous to her relations with her prime ministers. Their "advice", as in the Margaret–Townsend affair, is decisive. The Queen is no iconoclast.

Is she popular? Does she wish to be? Sarah Bradford ended her long biography with the words, "Elizabeth represents values which most people still recognise even if they do not either practise them or aspire to them themselves – courage, decency, and a sense of duty," to which I would add sagacity, courtesy and reasonableness. These are admirable qualities, but they are not specially lovable. Unlike her mother, she does not expect to be loved, and unlike her, she was probably more popular in her youth than in her older age, because then she represented vivacity and glamour, and today she represents stability. She refuses to be charismatic. Her reign has been a triumph of survival, but survival, as at Dunkirk, is only marginally triumphant. Her Golden Jubilee indicated that she is respected and liked, and that we are grateful to her, sometimes sorry for her, but the crowds were demonstrating more satisfaction than delight. They were pleased to be British, and pleased that she is the most British of us all. She is associated in our minds with patriotism, a declining and sometimes despised emotion, except in sport, since there have been no serious wars to stimulate it. We no longer sing "God Save the Queen" at the end of performances, unless she is there. But it would be unfair to imagine that she is sustained solely by custom, "like a picture on a chocolate box", as a social scientist wrote in 1976, "which gives pleasure to some, while others hardly think about it". Her activities add lustre to her position, although she is no longer regarded as a radiant personality. She has a talent to be amused. Like her mother, she looks happiest when leading in a winner. What is lacking is the spontaneous gesture, the unconventional, the daring, which alone can turn affection into love, as Diana demonstrated, and establish in people's minds a character that is not solely a royal character. It would be surprising if her vivacity were not worn down by duties that can only end with her death – for she has made it clear that she has no intention of abdicating – and by the personal sorrows which have blighted her recent years. She and her husband are permanencies, and their reputations are firm and honourable, unlike the kaleidoscopic images of her children, and that is a valuable achievement.

Tony Blair has made the monarchy temporarily secure, even though his Cabinet is said to contain a number of closet Republicans. He has shown great respect for the Queen. In September 2002, on returning from important talks with President Bush at Camp David, he flew not to London, but to Aberdeen, to report to her at Balmoral the outcome of his discussions. In his speech celebrating her golden wedding, he said, "You, ma'am, are a symbol of unity in a world of insecurity. You are our Queen. We respect and cherish you. You are simply the best of British." While this could be taken as prime-ministerial hyperbole on a joyful occasion, there is no doubt that New Labour has learnt to suppress its republican leanings. Public opinion, too, is supportive of the monarchy, though it fluctuates according to the emotions of the moment. A year before the Queen Mother died, 34 per cent were in favour of a Republic, on the day after her funeral, 12 per cent.

The extreme republican case has been put by Julie Burchill, as quoted by Ben Pimlott. Monarchy, she wrote, is a sign of decadence. It shows that a nation is living in its past. Only somnolent nations – the Dutch, the Scandinavians, the British – have kings and queens. The vital nations, she implied – the United States, Russia, China, Germany – have long discarded them. She went on, "To see a group of people, under-educated, inbred, possessing neither intelligence nor beauty...ruling all it surveys, is the kiss of death to a country." It has not yet killed this country for the simple reason that our royals do not rule it. It would be an intolerable violation of democracy to submit to an unelected monarch. The Queen does not make the laws: she simply signs them. She does not declare war: she consents to war being declared by her government, and then gives it her moral support. The

Republicans further argue that monarchy sets its seal on an antiquated class system. But does it not rise above all this? The hereditary peers could not be saved by the Crown's intervention, nor can the Queen prevent the slow democratisation of the Brigade of Guards, which is nominally under her command. The forces of meritocracy are far stronger than the traditions of the Crown. The argument that the monarchy costs too much is less heard now that the Queen pays tax on her private income and is seen to make economies. A president would cost just as much. Chirac lives in the Elysée in a style at least equal to the Queen's in her palaces. Besides, a president, elected every five years or so from a list of rival candidates, would bring with him or her a political past and a train of supporters, critics, enemies and possibly lovers who would cause far more trouble than our minor royals. What would be the president's powers? Who, indeed, would make a suitable president? The qualifications are current popularity, proved ability in a variety of difficult jobs, not too controversial a past, personal or political, and the ability to rise from esteem to distinction. Betty Boothroyd, the ex-Speaker, might qualify on these grounds. Richard Branson, the favourite candidate of the young, would refuse to stand. It is difficult to think of others. Is one necessary? We already have a president, the Queen.

The arguments in support of a monarchy can be given less negatively, on historical, emotional and practical grounds. History is not to be sneezed at. We are what we are because of what we have been, and the monarchy personifies our past. It is a fundamental element in our national identity. It satisfies a natural yearning for glamour and excess in impoverished times, and is a focus in prosperity. It makes us feel that we belong to something that matters. It impresses foreigners, whether as royal guests or tourists. Its patronage is of immense help to charities. It appeals to the sentimental in us – the little Princesses, the corgis, "Mummy", a photograph of Prince William about to kiss a girl, two beautiful heads in profile. It appeals to our more exalted emotions on the great occasions. The Queen's presence stamps them on our memories. Constitutionally, the monarchy is a still point in a revolving world. It is not a very important point, but it is a solid one. As my father wrote in his life of George V, explaining the King's passivity, "The appeal of hereditary monarchy is to stability rather than change, to continuity rather than experiment, to custom rather than to novelty, to safety rather than to adventure." Inertia in a monarch can be a national asset, although perhaps a dull one.

There is a constant susurration in favour of a simpler monarchy, one that is closer to the people's feelings and habits, and less expensive. From time to time we hear a demand for one based on the Scandinavian model, with bicycles and errant children, but this demand lacks precision. What exactly do we mean by it? Norway's monarchy can be taken as an example. In August 2001 Crown Prince Haakon fell in love with Mette-Marit Tiessom Holby, a bright and lovely girl who confessed to a tumultuous youth and already had a son four years old by a man convicted of drug charges. The King and Queen not only gave their consent to the marriage, but appeared on the palace balcony after the wedding with Mette's little boy at their side. His father was not invited. The crowd were delighted. Or take the Dutch royal wedding, six months later. Maxima Zorreguieta, a clever Argentinian beauty, married Crown Prince William Alexander. Conservatives complained that she was doubly unsuitable as a future Queen, because she was a Roman Catholic, and her father had been a Minister in a government which ruthlessly murdered thousands of its opponents. This father was also omitted from the wedding invitations, and the new

Princess agreed that her children would be brought up in the Dutch Reformed Church. Once again, the crowd were overjoyed. The polls showed that Maxima was more popular than Queen Beatrice herself. That is often the fate of queens whose sons marry beautiful commoners.

These two examples suggest that the Norwegians and Dutch are more willing to compromise with traditional moralities than the British. While we might accept Maxima as a bride for Prince William (because neither of her disadvantages was her fault), it is unlikely that we would greet Mette with the acclaim that the Norwegians afforded her. On the other hand, the Scandinavian royal families are not more powerful and scarcely more democratic than the British. King Harald of Norway, for instance, has a royal yacht and five State and five private residences. Norway is a constitutional monarchy, which, like our own, means the opposite of what it says. The King does not rule the country. He cannot overturn the decisions of his Ministers, but he is a symbol that means a great deal to his people. He is less formal than our Queen. He is seen to mingle with the crowds in a more relaxed way than our royal walkabouts. When there was a fuel shortage, his father, Olav V, "the People's King", travelled by public transport. Whatever the fuel crisis in Britain, the Queen would not do that, though she might curtail her journeys. The excuse would be Security, but the true reason would be that she has no need to enhance her popularity by unnecessary stunts. In the Netherlands, Queen Beatrix has no political power. Although laws are passed in her name, she has no veto on legislation, but has a weekly audience with her Prime Minister, and "approves" the appointment of other Ministers. That is all. She is deeply interested in politics, but keeps aloof. She makes minor changes in her conduct to keep Republicanism at bay. For instance, her children went to State schools, and when her son William succeeds to the throne, his nephews and nieces will not be called princes and princesses. One reason for her popularity is that she is always the first on the scene of any disaster. It is the same in Sweden, where the King's role is purely ceremonial, and he uses the royal palace at Stockholm only as an office. In short, the other European monarchies are not very different from our own. They face the same strains, the same criticisms, and keep going solely because the majority of their peoples want them. One can only tinker with monarchy up to a certain point. If it were bereft of all prestige, its showmanship would look absurd. It largely depends upon the Monarch's personality. If our Queen made a habit of shopping unescorted at Marks & Spencer, she would be mobbed and would not enjoy it. But when Queen Margrethe of Denmark goes shopping in Copenhagen, the people leave her alone and love her for it. In Britain, it is for the minor royals to link monarchy with the people on a human level.

There is room for only minor adjustments to our monarchy because many of its powers have been shredded already and its remaining functions are still needed. It would be sensible to abolish the Queen's Speech at the opening of Parliament, and substitute a statement of intent by the Prime Minister and an encouraging message, which the Queen could deliver from the throne. The ban on royals marrying Catholics, persons of other religions and divorced people should be lifted. The vestigial power to appoint prime ministers and dissolve Parliament could be formally abolished instead of being left to wither. The verses of the national anthem should be rewritten, and "Land of Hope and Glory" dropped except for Elgar's marvellous tune. The position of minor royals should be regularised. They cannot be expected to play the part of the ideal family, and it is uncertain what the public wants of them. They are needed to take the Queen's place on minor occasions, and they must be seen to earn their living in non-controversial ways or distance themselves from the Crown completely. It depends upon their own judgement in a difficult situation. If they remain royal, but behave like the rest of us, what is the point of them? If they cease to be royal, the whole edifice will lack a base.

Prince Harry is an example. He will never be insignificant, with his height and knobkerrie head of red hair. But what is he to do? He is now eighteen. He is cheerful, vigorous and fun-loving, cheekier than his brother, perhaps more adventurous, like Margaret to the young Elizabeth. It is said that he wishes to concern himself with some of his mother's charitable work, visiting the sick and homeless, and while that could be tough and challenging, it is not a career. He is not brilliant. He failed to reach his potential at Eton. He is most unlikely to succeed his brother on the throne. He must devise a strategy for his life, not leave its development to sporadic chance. The professions are not entirely closed to him. He could work for one of the Specialised Agencies of the United Nations, he could be an executive officer in one of his chosen charities, he could manage a large agricultural estate. Who knows, at eighteen, what one really wants to do? Whatever he does, he will be a model for other royals, and make a significant impact on his generation.

Few people now doubt the Prince of Wales's fitness to succeed his mother. He is a man of integrity and sensibility, with a love of nature and the arts. He has original ideas, and the courage to express them. Another man in his position might have shied away from people and theories that interested him, for fear that the Press would discover them and ridicule him. He never did. For a short time he was a national joke. No longer. He would bring to the monarchy a refreshing novelty and an articulate grace.

The difficulty is his relationship with Camilla Parker

Bowles. He loves her, and she him. Jonathan Dimbleby, his confidant, has written, "In her the Prince found the warmth, the understanding and the steadiness for which he had always longed, and had never been able to find with any other person." For five years after his marriage he tried to keep apart from her, but when it went irretrievably wrong, he returned to her. After Diana's death they became inseparable. Charles handled this difficult situation with the utmost tact. They began by appearing together at public functions, but arrived separately, mingled separately and left separately. Then they allowed themselves to be seen talking together, and then photographed together. Later they were shown walking hand in hand, and once the Prince was filmed lightly kissing her on the cheek in a row of other kissables. Finally, she was invited to Buckingham Palace by the Queen, and after the Jubilee they spent several days together at the Castle of Mey and Balmoral. These were all stages in her advance towards acceptability. It came to be recognised that Charles, who had often shared a roof with her at night, now shared the same ceiling. Early in 2003 he moved from St James's Palace into Clarence House, his grandmother's home for fifty years. Camilla was to live there too.

This did not disturb the public. But when it came to the possibility of their marriage, people reacted strangely. In a MORI poll of June 2000, 44 per cent of those questioned urged them to marry, and 33 per cent believed that they should continue as before, unmarried. The more significant result was that 71 per cent believed that Camilla should never become Queen. This was not because they thought ill of her personally – indeed, a great deal was said in her favour – but because, sentimentally, they considered that in their lifetimes they wanted only one Princess of Wales, Diana, and that Charles's remarriage should carry with it a sort of penalty, that Camilla should be denied the rank to which marriage entitled her, just as Wallis was denied the title of Royal Highness. Then there were the Church's objections. The memory of the Abdication, and Princess Margaret's renouncement of Peter Townsend under pressure from the Church, still hung heavily in older people's memories. Has the Church's attitude changed?

It has changed, but only slightly. Archbishop Carey declared that the marriage would create a crisis for the Church. In the cases of the Windsors and Peter Townsend, only one of each couple had been divorced – Wallis and Peter. Now both parties were divorced, and only one of them, Charles, was widowed, which made the prospect of his marriage to Camilla doubly reprehensible. The more orthodox clergy said that it would be akin to lifelong adultery, incompatible with the role of a future Supreme Governor of the Church of England. So the Church faced this difficulty, that while it implicitly condoned his living in sin with his mistress, it could not condone his marriage to her, which in the eyes of the lay public would make their union more respectable, and give comfort to the Prince's sons.

Public opinion on this issue will surely change, and Archbishop Williams is more likely to respond to that change than his predecessor. He has already declared himself agreeable to the remarriage of divorced persons in normal circumstances. Why not the royals too? If this is conceded, why should Camilla not become Queen? I foresee that opposition to this idea will soon subside. A morganatic marriage, in which the wife has no claim to the possessions or title of her husband, is a procedure unknown to the British constitution. It would isolate her as "Lady Camilla", without entitlement to Royal Highness. It would be an insult to both of them. Where would she be seated at the Coronation? How would visiting heads of state be expected to treat her? On some occasions she would be accepted as the King's wife, on others not. She would be a Consort without the dignity of rank, and bear to her dying day the stigma of illegitimacy. We should not expose this decent woman, and this man born and worthy to be King, to such humiliation. In February 2003 he wrote for the Journal of the Royal Society of Literature an essay on education, which contained these words: "In a world where the trite, the banal, the cliché and the commonplace are so dominant a part of our lives, we need even more to cherish, and to preserve and celebrate, the beauty, the solemnity and the harmony we inherit from the past." Imagine George V or VI, or Edward VIII, writing, unaided, a sentence like that, and feeling it so profoundly. These spasms of emotion do him, and the monarchy, great credit

He is not universally admired. There are accusations that he overplays his hand, and that he should follow his mother's example, by asking questions without suggesting the answers. But he cares too much to remain silent. If he sympathises strongly with the Tibetans for their treatment by the Chinese, he refuses to attend a banquet in honour of the Chinese Emperor, and lets it be known why. If he believes that the Government mishandled the foot-and-mouth crisis, he says so. In a private talk with the Prime Minister, he declares that farmers are treated worse than "blacks and gays", and the minute of their conversation is leaked. His letters to other ministers on a wide variety of topics arouse their fear that as King he may take the surviving royal prerogatives too literally, and interfere with government itself. He is respected for his candour, but his critics wish it were more muted. If he has strong views on policy, let him express them in unrecorded talks with ministers, but not bombard them with letters, because his sharp memos are circulated to other departments, and leak. He must not become a lobbyist. We are so accustomed to kings-in-waiting being playboys or nonentities that it comes as quite a shock to discover that we have a Prince who thinks, and, as Anthony Holden wrote as long ago as 1988, "has redefined the role of Prince of Wales".

The Queen herself has not been immune to criticism. The newspapers long ago discovered that blame and scandal is more eagerly absorbed by their readers than praise, of which a little goes a long way. There was, for instance, in the closing months of 2002, the extraordinary episode of Paul Burrell. He had been the Queen's favourite footman for ten years – loyal, chirpy, friendly, discreet – and then became Diana's butler and confidant, even to the extent of smuggling her lovers into Kensington Palace in the boot of his car. When she died, he took it on himself to save some of her letters and personal possessions that might have fallen into the wrong hands or been destroyed by Diana's family. In 1997, in the course of a long interview with the Queen, he told her what he had done, and she assented by silence. It seemed to both of them a matter of small importance. Five years later he was charged with purloining these objects and selling them for his own profit, but at the trial the police could produce no evidence of a sale. The Queen was in Canada when the trial began, and reading of it in the newspapers, she decided to help Burrell by revealing to the court what he had told her, adding that she had raised no objection to what he had done. In face of this evidence from such a source, the trial was immediately abandoned. This did not prevent the *Independent* from publishing a leading article headed, "A case that may inflict serious damage on the monarch and monarchy". The Queen, it said, should have realised the importance of what Burrell had told her, and revealed it sooner. This was unfair. The police were responsible for the mistrial, not her

The public relish such aborted scandals, but soon shake

them off. By and large, the monarchy enjoys their support. As the Duke of Edinburgh said in a recent television interview, "A young Queen and a young family are infinitely more newsworthy and amusing...But I think people have grown more accustomed to us." In time, as love grows a bit cold, it is replaced by a sort of veneration. It has been so in the past, particularly in the case of Queen Victoria. The monarchy has survived even the most unworthy monarchs. When George IV died, *The Times*, in a famous obituary, wrote of him, "There never was an individual less regretted by his fellow creatures than this deceased King. What eye has wept for him? What heart has heaved one throb of unmercenary sorrow?" Yet he was succeeded, without protest, by William IV, a monarch of even less significance. Today we have no comparable problem. If our royal family is no longer glamorous, they are still the centre of glamorous occasions. If Trafalgar Square is the focus of protest, Buckingham Palace is the focus of acclamation. The royals are associated in our minds with institutions of which we are proud – the Royal Navy, the RAF, the Royal Mail, the RHS, The RSPCA, the Jubilee Line and much else – and they gain in public respect from that association. Nobody will ever stand for hours in the rain to watch a Prime Minister or Archbishop drive to St Paul's, but, inexplicable as it may be, they always will for Kings and Queens.

# INDEX

Burma, 78
Burney, Fanny, 36
Burrell, Paul, 140
Bush, President George W., 131
Butler, R.A. ('Rab'), 59, 87

Caernarvon Castle, 70–1
Callaghan, James, 54
Cambridge University, 87
Canada, 28, 79
Cape Town, 23–4
Carey, George (Archbishop of Canterbury), 138
Carrington, Lord, 53, 56–7
Cawston, Richard, 68
Ceausescu, Nicolae (President of Romania), 73
Chamberlain, Neville, 10
Channon, Sir Henry ('Chips'), 9
Charles, Prince of Wales see Wales, Charles, Prince of
Charteris, Sir Martin, 28, 37, 52, 60
Cheam School, 26, 84
Checketts, Sir David, 86
China, 75, 139
Chirac, Jacques, (President of France), 132
Church of England, 128–9, 138–9
Churchill, Sir Winston: relations with George VI, 11, 12, 17; on Princess Elizabeth aged two, 19; at her wedding, 27; receives the Order of the Garter, 50, his second premiership, 50; relations with Queen Elizabeth II, 49–52; resigns, 52
Clarence House, 40, 137
Clark, Sir Kenneth, 61
Clarke, Helen, 121
Colville, Sir John ('Jock'), 22, 50–1, 52
Commonwealth: Queen dedicates herself to, 24; her titles at

Coronation, 29; Lusaka Conference, 56–7; her influence on, 56–7; travels to, 77–81; Africa 79–81; Games, 124–5. See Australia, Canada, New Zealand.
Cook, Robin, 117, 118–9
Coronation of Queen Elizabeth II (1953), 29–33
Cranwell, 90
Crawford, Marion, 19–20, 26
Crossman, Richard, 57–8

Danish monarchy, 135
Dartmouth, 90
Dartmouth, Raine, 93
Diana, Princess of Wales: childhood and education, 93; engaged to Prince Charles, 94–5; wedding, 95–6; honeymoon, 96; failing marriage, 96–7; dances with Wayne Sleep, 97; cares for sick, 97; tapes and television, 98–9; divorce, 99; post-divorce popularity, 103–4, 119; AIDS and mines, 104; death, 104; funeral, 106–7; her legacy, 108, 137
Dimbleby, Jonathan, 76, 83–4, 89, 94, 98–9, 137
Douglas-Home, Sir Alec (Lord Home), 59, 128
Douglas-Home, Charles, 80
Duke of Edinburgh's Award, the, 44, 123

Eccles, David, 31
Eden, Anthony, 42, 51, 60
Edinburgh, Philip, Duke of: engagement and marriage, 25–7; in Paris and Canada with the Queen, 27–8; at the Coronation, 30–2, 44; his role and character, 43–5, 67; BBC film, 69; and Prince Charles, 83, 85; speech

about the Queen, 117; on Jubilee tour, 123; his future, 141

Edward VII, King, 2

Edward VIII, King see Windsor, Duke of

Edward, Prince (Earl of Wessex), 102, 111–13

Eisenhower, President Dwight D., 50, 60

Elgar, Sir Edward, 125, 135

Elizabeth II, Queen: Life: childhood, 18–20; in wartime, 21–2; to South Africa, 22–5; engagement and marriage, 25–7; visit to France, 27–8; Canada and USA, 27–9; Coronation, 29–33; Prince of Wales investiture, 70–2; Commonwealth tour (1953), 78; 1977 Jubilee, 81; death of Diana, 105–6; TV address on Diana, 106; post-Diana life, 113–4; Golden Jubilee, 122–6, 130; Political role: attention to, 49; relations with Churchill, 49–52; with other Prime Ministers, 52,53–7; her political experience, 52–3, 117; relations with Thatcher, 54–7; with Labour Ministers, 57–8; her prerogatives, 58–9,117-8; royal finances, 61–4; role in Scotland, 53,117-8; New Labour attitude to monarchy, 131; Non-political roles: Colonel of Grenadier Guards, 21; character of her Court, 37, 46–7; investitures and parties, 65–6; tours of the country, 66–7; state visits to England, 73–4; her visits abroad, 74–6; receives ambassadors, 114–5; popularity, 129–30. See Jubilees Commonwealth: dedicates her life to, 24–5; South African tour, 22–5; Lusaka Conference, 56–7;

Influence in Africa, 78–81; India and Pakistan, 118–9; Commonwealth Games, 124–5; See Australia, Canada, New Zealand

Family: her parents, 5, 40; Charles and Anne born, 28; the Margaret-Townsend affair, 41–3; royal finances, 61–4; her art-collection, 62; BBC films of, 68–9, 101–2; attitude to Charles, 83, 101; to Diana, 95; to Prince Philip, 43–4, 117; reaction to Charles–Diana split, 99; It's a Knockout, 102; Diana's death, 105–6, 128; trouble with minor royals, 113; Paul Burrell affair, 140

Character: her appearance, 35; influence of her father, 5, 40; in childhood, 19; and adolescence, 22–25; her interests, 38; racing, 38; courage, 30; religion, 39, 128–9; Altrincham criticisms, 45–8; her reticence in public, 35–6, 48, 67–8; her speeches, 53; humour, 58, 68; character in later life, 115–6, 130; 'mistakes', 127; no scandals, 128

Elizabeth, Queen Mother: help to George VI, 9–10; character, 14–15, 103, 110; in wartime, 15–6; as Queen Mother, 40; the Simpson affair, 41; the Townsend affair, 42; in old age, 103, 110; her death, 109–10

Euston, Lady, 37

Everest, Mount, 30

Fagan, Michael, 39

Falklands War, 97, 127

Fellowes, Sir Robert, 93, 106

Fiji, 78

Fisher, Geoffrey (Archbishop of Canterbury), 31–2, 42, 46